GW00499734

Bleak Hotel

The Hollywood saga of
The White Hotel

BLEAK HOTEL

D. M. THOMAS

QUARTET

First published in 2008 by
Quartet Books Limited
A member of the Namara Group
27 Goodge Street, London W1T 2LD

A catalogue record for this book
is available from the British Library

ISBN   978 0 7043 7145 3

Typeset by Antony Gray
Printed and bound in Great Britain by
T J International Ltd, Padstow, Cornwall

For Ross,
who has found his own way
with strength and grace

Acknowledgements

A longer version of the section 'Ex Directory' first appeared, under the title 'Last Words', in the *Guardian* on June 10 2006.

The poem 'Again' was first published in my collection *Not Saying Everything* (Bluechrome, 2006).

The poem 'Rubbing Against You' was first published in my collection *Dear Shadows* (Fal Publicaitons, 2004).

I am very grateful to Philippe Mora and Susan Potter for kind permission to quote from their emails to me in 2005–6.

My thanks also to my wife Angela for her wise and thoughtful suggestions.

Contents

ONE

Big Dreams

> *Soon to be a major film.*

from Penguin Books' back cover, 1981

Susan Potter, head of JOA Productions, California,
to D. M. Thomas
April 2006

Hi Don: We ARE coming your way. We leave a week from Sunday – May 7, arriving in London on May 8. We shall go to Cannes on May 16– 28. Pushing sales at that time . . .

Do you think you and Angela would like to come up to London for a day/night. Do let us know. We'd love to see you – celebrate the FINALLY HAPPENING phase of this long journey. Celebrate your brilliant novel. Celebrate YOU!

Cheers, dahlink . . .

Susan

In 1981 I published a novel, *The White Hotel*, which unexpectedly aroused in readers a passionate admiration or equally passionate distaste. Within a few months of its publication, I received an offer to option the film rights.

My novel's heroine, Lisa, born in Odessa in 1890, walks a tightrope between Eros and Thanatos. She has a great gift for happiness and pleasure, but is tortured by the suffering of others and the intuition that great suffering will come to her. She is right, for in 1941 she becomes caught up in the massacre of Jews at Babi Yar in Kiev. The 'white hotel' of her sexual fantasy, written for her analyst Sigmund Freud, encompasses the extremes of pleasure and pain, joy and grief. The novel is complex in structure, moving from Lisa's sexual fantasy in verse to a prose expansion of it, then to Freud's 'intellectual' fantasy, to the nightmarish 'real' fantasy of Babi Yar, and finally to a spiritual fantasy. Each section is stylistically different. The novel therefore poses serious challenges for a film maker.

The present book traces, from the author's limited perspective, the story of twenty-seven years of the non-making of the film, 1981–2008. It is not important whether a novel becomes a film; often the result is unsatisfactory anyway. And long delays are not infrequent. Nevertheless, the history of this particular non-making is an extraordinary one; it involves years of passion, obsession, alleged financial skulduggery, hatred and vengeance. At one point, the film rights were sold for one dollar, though for the next seven years I was kept in ignorance of this; at another, the film looked set fair to be made, but an improbable war stopped it. I was sued for millions of dollars, and feared to lose my home. One of the main protagonists fell dead of a heart attack, in mid-life, when apparently in perfect health. His partner ascribed his death to a venomous legal battle over the rights. His legal opponent queried in a New York law court whether in fact he had really died – implying that he might have faked his own death to escape justice.

Inevitably the story of the non-movie blends into my own life-story and that of the people closest to me. One of the main though half-unconscious inspirations for my novel was my mistress, then wife, and always Muse, Denise. She died of cancer, aged fifty-three, in 1998; but just as the dead and the living are mixed up in Lisa's fantasy, so my relationship with her did not end with her death. 'For nothing in the white hotel but love / Is offered at a price we can afford'. I was caught up, as collateral damage, in the brutal legal conflict which has been going on for almost a decade; it was costly to me, both financially and, even more, emotionally and creatively, draining my energies. But those lines of Lisa's about love remain the enduring truth.

Glass Fibre Optics

I sometimes imagine a *White Hotel* movie of all the talents – everyone who has ever been *almost* involved in the project. Great directors would have only three or four minutes of screen time to show their genius. The audience would have to guess . . . 'I'm sure that scene with the hunchback voyeur was Lynch . . . ' 'No, for me it had a Slavic touch – Kusturica, I'd say.' Likewise with the screenplay: 'The soft-shuffle dance at Babi Yar – that's a terrific Potter moment!' As for the innumerable actors and actresses, most would be forced to take tiny roles, and would play them brilliantly . . . 'The concierge – wasn't that Hopkins?' ' – Yes, and for my money he stole the film.' 'The chambermaid in the white hotel – I'm sure that was Juliette Binoche.' ' – Oh, I didn't notice; but the baker's wife, in the dining room, was Barbra Streisand . . . ' There'd be Oscars for thirty or forty directors and actors, an endless procession to the podium.

The story goes that it was Barbra Streisand who started it off, not long after the book created something of a publishing sensation as the 'sleeper novel' of 1981. Someone remarked to her at a party that she ought to look for an intelligent, demanding role, and suggested *The White Hotel*. She went straight to Keith Barrish, producer of *Endless Love*, and said, 'Keith, you owe me a favour. I want you to buy *The White Hotel*.' So he bought it for her; at least, an option.

Bernardo Bertolucci told me, years later, Streisand had invited him to her Hollywood mansion to discuss the film over dinner. Gold dinner service – butler – the works. She said, 'Bernardo, there's just one thing bothering me: how are we going to deal with all the sex?'

'Well, Barbra, I have this idea for glass fibre optics to enter the woman's vagina.'

A moment's silence, then: 'Let me show you the house.'

And she never spoke of *The White Hotel* to him again.

That was Bertolucci's story. There may have been some Italianate exaggeration. He would come and go in the saga over the next twenty years; but soon, in this early phase, Mark Rydell, who had recently directed *On Golden Pond*, was seemingly in the director's chair. A meeting with him in New York, when I was there promoting the US paperback, was arranged in 1982. At that time, *The White Hotel* was number one on the British paperback list for six successive weeks, and number two in the States, beaten for first place by *Gorky Park*. It was a fair achievement for such a complex novel, with a long erotic poem early in the narrative, and at its heart a quasi-Freudian analysis; and had a film been made then, as the Penguin cover proclaimed, I don't think the producer would have been struggling to find leads. (It's so long ago, it wouldn't surprise me if Barrish and Rydell were thinking of Betty Grable and Errol Flynn.)

At our meeting in his plush, sky-rise apartment, Rydell seemed distracted, perhaps even embarrassed; becoming animated only when he rushed to the next room to speak several times on the phone about some other business. I think he already knew he was not going to direct the film. If, for a brief time, he conjured up scenes from my novel in his filmic imagination, those imagined images faded back into the limbo of unmade Rydell movies.

A Different Movie

I dream of Denise, my dead (second) wife. For thirteen years we lived together thinking we were divorced, and that this was good since it relieved the pressure of marriage, but in fact we were still legally married. A lawyer fouled up the divorce papers, or the court fouled up; but in any case at the end we were grateful we were still married.

As often happens, she wakes me up after I've dreamt of her, to prevent me from forgetting the encounter. We have this ongoing life, even after another marriage and a divorce, and now another marriage. Angela, my fourth and last wife, so wise for a woman in her late thirties, understands. In this dream, a friend who has had an affair with Denise has written a moving, lyrical account of a day they spent together. In real life he doesn't write, scarcely even reads, but I'm impressed by the intense emotion of the scene, as he describes it. Denise assures me, with a smile, she had better times with me; but still, I am jealous. Jealous, seven years after her death, and almost nine years after we last made love!

Though she appears only briefly, her presence is tangible, real, in a way that other dream figures are not. All the emotions I feel about her and associate with her are present.

Big Dreams

We're like a producer and a director, in my unconscious, scene by scene creating a movie of our life together after her death.

I find it increasingly hard to sleep through the night. Either I can't get to sleep at all, or I wake in the middle of the night with a raging thirst from having drunk too much wine. Or, in this case, Denise wakes me. Leaving Angela asleep – the deep sleep of the young – I pad downstairs in my dressing gown and make tea. Whenever I drink tea I have to eat something; so I bring a tin of water biscuits and the butter dish to the table. Whenever I am eating something – if I'm alone – I have to be reading. I drink, butter and eat water biscuits, and read. Little buttery biscuit follows little buttery biscuit. It's a habit that brings back my father to me. On Saturday nights in his late teens, we children were told, he would come home late with the *Football Herald*; his mother would have left a flask of tea and a plate of freshly baked saffron buns. And dad would drink tea, munch buns, and devour the local rugby news. His eyes would not leave the newsprint. Until he reached out his hands and there were no saffron buns left. It's always made me feel warmly close to him, that image.

And if he were still alive, rather than forty five years dead, he would smile to see me scoffing water biscuits and reading.

Our kitchen table is like a battlefield where time has erased the mud, trenches and craters. Like green, sleepy Beaumont Hamel or Thiepval on the Somme. Vanished are those violent dramas between Denise and me that sometimes lasted all night: the emptying whisky bottle, the overwhelmed ashtrays, the repetitive abuse of me (most of it richly deserved). My sister thinks we should buy a new table, because this one is so scarred and stained; but I wouldn't change it for the world. It's our white hotel, so much passion, excitement, destruction.

Texans

After Barbra Streisand's apparent reluctance to contemplate glass fibre optics, Keith Barrish let our option agreement lapse. Warner Brothers made a fairly small and half-hearted offer. I agreed with my London agent, Andrew Hewson, that I had probably no alternative but to accept it.

Then, in February 1985, a throbbing, melodic American voice on the phone burst into my small world of sleepy rural Hereford, on the English-Welsh border. 'Mr Thomas? My name is Bobby Geisler. I and my partner John Roberdeau would like to know if the rights to *The White Hotel* are available.'

'Well, yes, they could be.'

'We love your book. We think we can make a great movie of it. John and I would be happy to fly anywhere in the world at a moment's notice to talk to you about it.'

I liked the way his voice caressed the title of my book, reverentially, as though stroking a lover or a shiny new Porsche. I was going to be passing through London, on my way back from somewhere or other, in a few days. 'I could meet you for an hour – no more – at the Great Western Hotel at Paddington Station in London. Four o'clock.'

'We'll be there.'

I rang Andrew. An upright Scot, he said, 'But I've already said yes to Warner Brothers.'

'Sod that, we haven't signed anything! They've got no plans. Let's hear what these people have to say.'

So Andrew and I met, in the seedy lounge of the decaying hotel of a great terminus, where many of the journeys of my life have begun or ended; and we waited for the mysterious Americans.

They burst in like a small whirlwind, Geisler in front. 'D. M. Thomas? I'm Bobby Geisler, and this is my partner John

Roberdeau. It's so wonderful to meet you! Thank you for agreeing to see us.'

They looked to be in their early thirties. Geisler was round-faced, with thinning fair hair that streamed out like a sun-disc; red braces held up baggy trousers. Roberdeau was good-looking, trim and neat, an altogether quieter, more businesslike presence. We tried to order drinks, but the licensing laws forbade it; we had tea and biscuits instead. Our visitors were so quintessentially, exuberantly American – especially Geisler – that I hardly can escape the words 'red suspenders', 'pants' and 'cookies', instead of their English equivalents. The odd couple exuded reverence for *The White Hotel* – Bobby again caressing the title silkily. 'We want to create a movie, Don, that will do justice to your great book, and we think we can do it.'

'We know we can do it,' John corrected.

' – We *know* we can do it!' Bobby's faced glowed with rapture. 'We have an idea for how it will open, and we want to pass it by you. The opening chords of the overture to *Don Giovanni*' – his arms spread like a conductor's – 'those crashing chords, as we see Lisa in the train, travelling to the white hotel . . . The music perfectly wedded to the poetry and the images . . . It can be *wonderful!*'

Well, yes, it could be, I thought, already drawn to these enthusiasts. 'And we would like you to write the screenplay,' John said.

'We think that's important,' Bobby added. 'You know your great book better than anyone. We want to work very closely with you at every stage.'

I had no experience of writing screenplays; but the idea appealed to me. I thought I was sufficiently far from the writing of the novel to be able to see it afresh and not get bored. They left us, after their torrential sales pitch, to fly back to New York. Andrew and I were a little dazed. He felt rather more sceptical than I, but quickly agreed that we should test them out, see what sum they would offer for a three year option. We could ask for fifty thousand dollars up front, he suggested. I said no, let's ask for a hundred. If they were as keen as they claimed and appeared, they might say okay; and if not, we could come down to fifty thousand.

I caught the slow, Adlestrop-stopping train, through rolling meadows and woods, back to Hereford. In a couple of days their answer came: 'We accept'.

They said later they'd thought of beating us down to fifty thousand, then thought, Hell no, we'll show them we're serious.

A Way to Read Russian Novels

There were events in that period which made movie rights seem very trivial.

'Dad, I think I'm about to be charged with rape!' It was Sean's voice, shrill with fear. I was in the hall of my small semi-detached house close to the River Wye and Hereford Cathedral; Denise and Ross were in the living room watching TV. Two years previously my loving, long suffering first wife, Maureen, had left me. I and my new/old family (Denise and I had been lovers for twenty years) were still adjusting to living together. We would soon be moving to Cornwall, where we'd recently bought an old Coach House.

I composed myself. He must be exaggerating. 'Why, what's happened?'

'I took a copy of my novel around to' – I'm not allowed to say her name. Her identity is protected. I'll call her Rachel. ' – Rachel's flat, and we made love. It was just normal, just like it used to be; but afterwards she got upset, she cried, and I walked out. I know I shouldn't have done that, I should have stayed and talked. A few minutes ago, I had a call from her father, and he said he was sending the police round to charge me with rape. I keep expecting them any minute. I didn't rape her, dad!'

'I know that.' I really knew that.

'I guess because our relationship was in its last stages, and I walked out when she was upset, she felt used. She must have gone straight to her father.'

I tried to calm him down, saying it was probably just an empty threat. He cut in with, 'There's someone at the door; I think they're here.'

'Call me back.' We rang off. I went back into the living room, dazed, and told them what was happening. Ross was ten at the time; I imagine he didn't know what rape was.

We waited. After an hour or two the phone rang again. Sean. 'I'm at the police station; I've been charged with rape.'

I travelled up to London to watch him appear at a Magistrates' Court. The court dealt with one or two trivial offences, then I saw him, dressed in his only suit, looking terribly young and vulnerable, led up from the cells to answer the charge of 'Rape'. The word struck a chill through me. Rape is one of those charges where one immediately assumes guilt. I felt everyone in the court would have an image of a masked man with a knife leaping on a girl on a dark street, dragging her into the bushes, and raping her. But Sean and Rachel had been lovers – and in love – for two or three years. Their relationship had been slowly and spasmodically breaking up for the past few months. I wondered how the law could decide who, if anyone, was to blame in the last throes of a once passionate relationship. It wanted Freud to investigate it, not a detective.

The police opposed bail, on the grounds that he might seek to interfere with the alleged victim. He was sent on remand to the Scrubs. I spent frantic days, in consultation with Sean's friends, finding him a good solicitor. I travelled up again to see him in the Scrubs, and later in Brixton. And arranged through his friends a constant supply of cigarettes and books. His stay in prison was educational, in the sense that there he read most of the great Russian novels.

He shared a cell with a black guy, a genuine murderer – who was nice to him and whom he got to like. Somehow he survived the prisoners' hatred of 'sex offenders'. I couldn't bear to think of him banged up for twenty three hours of each day. It was as if I myself were in that cell. With my claustrophobia, I knew I could not stand it. Denise visited him too, and wrote to him, trying to keep his spirits up. Highly intelligent and intuitive, yet somehow inhibited when writing, she put a great effort into her letters to him, trying to reach across the divide caused by her having been 'the other woman' during his child-hood and teens ; indeed, till only a couple of years before, when his mother left me, sensibly, for a better, faithful marriage.

Rachel's parents, who were rich and influential, had an injunction slapped on Sean's novel. The police officer who had questioned him had read it; and pointed out that it contained an account of a rape. This showed, he argued, that Sean had been planning the rape.

Just as *Crime and Punishment* showed that Dostoevsky was planning to murder an old woman.

In discussions with the shrewd Jewish lawyer his friends and I found, I learned some of the case against him. Rachel had said to a girlfriend, 'I don't quite know what rape is, but I think Sean may have raped me.' A genuine victim of rape, I felt, would certainly know she had been raped. Rachel had been unmarked. It was basically her word against his.

At the last Old Bailey appeal against the refusal of bail, a judge granted it. The condition was that he live outside London, with me, and never visit London. I almost cried when I heard of this reprieve; and again when his friends told me on the phone he had banged his head with his hands when they'd brought the good news to him. I had to go to Hereford police station and show the deeds of my house to prove I could afford the £50,000 bond.

He had spent two months in prison. I knew how emotional

he would be, travelling through the middle of lush England, the quiet green 'Adlestrop' landscape, on his first day of freedom. Meeting his train, I was excited and moved; he made to come forward and hug me, and I wanted it; but some maddening reticence and reserve made me forestall it with a handshake. I instantly regretted it.

It was another nine months before the case came to trial. We were now living in Cornwall; and on the last day before we would have to travel up to London, we took him to Kynance Cove on the Lizard. It was a beautiful summer day, and the cove was at its most bewitching. We watched him stand alone on the white beach, sun sparkling on the water, the high serpentine cliffs. He said he wondered if he would see it again. He thought he would commit suicide if he was found guilty.

I met Maureen, Sean's mother, in London; we stayed with relatives of hers, and each day went together to the Old Bailey. Maureen, of course, was as sick with worry as I. On the first morning, photographers leapt out from the shadows in front of us and their cameras flashed. If there was a guilty verdict, the fact that he was my son would make it big news. We met Sean's counsel, Ronald Thwaites QC. He asked me not to go into court, in case he decided to call me as a witness. I spent each day of the trial, until the fourth and penultimate, pacing the corridors or smoking outside – waiting for Maureen or Sean's friends to fill me in on what had happened.

At the conclusion of Rachel's evidence, a photographer was overheard saying on the phone, 'She's admitted having been a heroin addict; that's it, we may as well go home.' I clutched desperately at every bit of hopeful news or gossip. By all accounts – insofar as these could be trusted, as they were from our side – Sean stood up well, being open and truthful about his faults and mistakes. Thwaites decided not to call me, and indeed there was little I could have said, apart from describing

Sean's panic and his obvious – to me – innocence on the fateful evening. Some of their love letters were read out. I was in court for the final addresses. The prosecuting counsel, a dry man more used to arguing complicated financial cases than even more complex psychosexual ones, said the jury, having heard the love letters, might well consider this a rather sad case. Thwaites, very assured, said there was really no case: they had been lovers, the accused did not threaten her with a weapon, and she showed no signs of forced sex. So the Thursday ended.

Next morning Sean was late arriving in court. My heart thumped. What if his nerve had failed and he'd done a bunk? Then he breezed in, and Thwaites threw up his arms in mixed exasperation and relief. The judge summed up in what seemed too balanced a way for my peace of mind, and the jury retired in mid-morning. Thwaites said he was optimistic – he'd seen a female member of the jury smile at him.

I'd decided I couldn't go in for the verdict. Within an hour the jury was back. I waited hopefully for word. Surely such a speedy decision could only mean an acquittal. But no, they'd asked the judge for a definition of 'reckless' behaviour. Panic assailed me. I rang home from a callbox; Denise and Ross too were waiting anxiously. 'Nothing yet; I'm afraid they're going to get him for recklessness.'

Shortly after a lunch I couldn't touch, the jury was back with a verdict. I waited in a kind of basement back-entrance. I saw police move in quietly; presumably to stop an affray if he were found guilty. I was sick with dread. The silence seemed to go on for ages, increasing the dread. It was a guilty verdict for sure, and the defence was calling character evidence. Then I heard a roar, and a few seconds later a clatter as his friends came bursting down the steps towards me, grinning broadly. I burst into tears.

I cried again when I gave Denise the news. 'Not guilty',

through sobs. I heard her shout to Ross upstairs at home – and she had a powerful shout: 'ROSS! NOT GUILTY!'

Later, Sean spoke to her, and urged her to jump on a train and come up for the celebration dinner. But she would never have made it; the trains from Cornwall to London Paddington are scarcely faster than a century ago. She contented herself with taking a bottle of sherry around to our neighbours, telling them what we had been going through, and getting blind drunk.

As did I and all of us at a Covent Gardens restaurant. Sean was in witty, sparkling form, making speeches and proposing endless toasts. Some reporters from the tabloid press had promised to pay for the dinner; but now, without a story, they baulked at the £700 bill. I paid it. I didn't care.

I returned to my new and quiet life in Cornwall, writing about Russian poets with complex love problems; and Sean resumed his bohemian Grub Street life in London. His identity was legally protected too; but he eventually decided to write about his horrific experience in a magazine, as a first step in the recovery process. It would take him many years, though, to recover fully. Even more years to feel he had taken from the experience something positive – in addition to reading *War and Peace* and *Anna Karenina*.

Anna and Vronsky

Anna, in a modern, feminist context, could well have accused Vronsky of rape. Tolstoy doesn't describe the actual seduction and love making, but one can assume she struggled, weakly, before giving way to his and her desires. Afterwards, tortured by guilt at breaking her vows, she must have wondered why it had happened, against her conscience; and it would be easier to assume he had overpowered her. Vronsky was looking down at her, after, as a murderer with an axe looks down at the body of his victim. So, guilt written all over him.

Vronsky is in prison on remand. Tolstoy again: 'No man truly understands the State until he has been in prison.' At the sensational trial, all eyes are on the distinguished officer and the tragic, weeping wife and mother. It is his word against hers; for there were no marks indicating violence, and Anna is too honest to claim he threatened her with his revolver, or that she feared he might use it. The jury, loath to send a man to prison for years when there is no evidence, acquits. Women's groups protest about the low conviction rate for rape, pointing out that no woman *ever* wrongfully accuses a man of this crime.

Anna and Vronsky are convinced they have both spoken the truth. They feel aggrieved and ashamed.

They are further tortured by still loving each other. Vronsky seeks death on a foreign battlefield; Anna suffers a breakdown, is divorced by her husband, but keeps her son.

Chuck me

Through 1987 Geisler and Roberdeau called me frequently with enthusiastic reports on progress. Geisler would say, in his round, reverential voice, 'Don, we have the extremely wonderful news that Fedorico Gonzalo' – I make up these names, because I don't remember the real ones – 'has agreed to work with us. Fedorico is by far the most visionary and imaginative and profound and poetic and altogether amazing cameraman in the business. We're so lucky to have him join our team . . . Or 'Don, John and I have spoken to Robert Forester, who heads the Harlem Ballet, the most amazing company of dancers in America. You probably saw them in James Paraday's movie "Ice Blink of Roses". Robert wants to be involved in *The White Hotel*!' Bobby never failed to caress the title – just as he was also caressing the magical names, Fedorico Gonzalo, or Robert Forester, or whatever. 'We are assembling a company of stars who are committed and who will do justice to your great novel.'

Big Dreams

I had written my first draft of the screenplay; making sure I began with the crashing chords of *Don Giovanni*. As I sent them extracts, they responded mostly with praise . . . 'We think that's a thrilling image, Don' . . . 'We love this scene . . . ' along with tentative suggestions for improvements. When I'd finished the second draft I sent it to Irene Webb, of the William Morris Agency, who were looking after the rights. She responded with 'brilliant'. I assumed, allowing for Hollywood inflation, she thought it pretty decent.

By coincidence, Geisler and Roberdeau were to be in Paris at the same time as I was to be there running a writers' workshop for a society of bored expatriate American women. Bobby and John greeted me warmly in an expensive restaurant, where they introduced me to Joe, a friend. Pumping my hand, he said he was a big fan of my book. He'd been reading my screenplay. Lulled by wine, his amiably smiling face, and his tone which hadn't changed from his eulogy of my novel, I didn't at first realise what was happening. I wondered why Bobby and John were looking down at their plates, moving bits of food around. Slowly I gathered that Joe thought my screenplay was complete crap.

He left early, still smiling, pumping my hand again; and I sat on, stunned, with the complicit and now largely silent producers. It was no surprise to be told, on my return to England, that they were hiring someone else, the historian Charles ('Chuck') Mee, to write the screenplay. They had decided to chuck me for Chuck Mee. He was handicapped, stricken with polio in his childhood; but they moved with him all around Europe hunting for locations and standing at his shoulder as he typed away. They seemed to have endless financial resources for research. Texan oil money, I gathered.

Showscan

Though my screenplay had been buried, Geisler and Roberdeau continued to dream, night and day, of the flying wombs
and breasts of my novel. Their other obsession was the brilliant
and reclusive director Terrence Malick. After directing *Bad
Lands* (1973) and *Days of Heaven* (1978), Malick had disappeared from the movie world. Geisler and Roberdeau
dreamed of tempting him back with my novel. I can imagine
Bobby's approach: 'We think the combination of the filmic
genius of Terry Malick and Don Thomas's amazing novel
would lead to a movie of breathtaking and beautiful and
visionary resonance. John Roberdeau and I are willing to drop
everything and fly to see you . . . '

In reality, their obsession and involvement with Malick was
much deeper than I knew. I only knew what they told me –
which was that Malick was not to be tempted by *The White
Hotel*. 'The boys', as I started to call them, turned instead to
Bernardo Bertolucci. They adored *Last Tango in Paris*, considering it one of the greatest films of the recent past. It seemed
he loved my novel, having already been involved with it in its
Streisand days.

Bertolucci, they said, had his own vision of the film and
would want to develop a screenplay that would place more
emphasis on Freud.

A message came from Bobby and John: 'We would like
you and Bernardo to fly to New York by Concorde to see a
demonstration of a new movie process called Showscan. We
think it has amazing potential for showing *The White Hotel*
with maximum impact.' I wasn't reluctant to break from writing
to fly by Concorde. I appreciated the incidental luxuries the
boys provided with such spendthrift generosity. It took me
four times as long to crawl by train to London, then to Heath-
row, as to reach from there to New York. Bertolucci and I were

whisked off by limo to a luxury hotel. And from there to a theatre showing Showscan.

The Showscan process projects 70mm film at an accelerated rate of 60 frames per second – which approximates to the speed with which the human eye perceives an image. The result, according to a recent advertisement: *'You're racing through the desert in a 4-wheel drive truck, doing 100 miles an hour. And all you can see is dirt and dust flying off the truck in front of you. Suddenly, a speeding 4-by-4 swerves directly in your path. You jam your foot down hard on the brake and prepare for impact . . . and then you remember, it's only a movie.*

'When the image is so real you can't tell it's a motion picture, it must be Showscan . . .'

Or you may not be able to tell it's a motion picture because you're sitting in a normal cinema. Showscan requires specially adapted cinemas. Bertolucci and I, and Geisler and Roberdeau, and many others, were in the first – and possibly the last – of such. We jammed our feet on the brakes in deserts, and sped down terrifying Big Dippers. When we emerged into the afternoon light of the Big Apple, Bobby and John collared us. Bobby enthused, 'Isn't it just incredible! Can you imagine how the sexual fantasies in the white hotel will look in Showscan?'

'Oh boy! That'll be quite somethin'!' John chuckled. They peered anxiously at Bernardo. 'What do you think, Bernardo?'

'I'm nauseous.' And he scuttled off to find a men's room.

We flew back to Europe, and I never heard another word about Showscan. And soon, very suddenly, the boys were having second thoughts about Bertolucci as director. They had taken another look at *Last Tango in Paris*, and decided it was overrated. And he wanted too much Freud.

They naturally gave me their version of events. It could be he asked for too much money; or he dropped them instead of their dropping him. Anyway, he was out of the picture. Just before he won an Oscar for The *Last Emperor*. Impeccable timing.

Now they were going for a homely hometown American boy. David Lynch.

Ex Directory

Trips abroad like that were welcome breaks from a largely lonely existence. Having come back 'home' to Cornwall, where I'd spent most of my early life, I found a distinctly unsociable atmosphere, far different from the warm working-class village life of my childhood. Of course that warm life still went on – elsewhere. Denise, Ross and I were now in the middle-class – mostly non-Cornish – world, but felt like misfits. We didn't belong to the yachting set, or the golfing set, or the arty set of Penzance and St Ives.

One evening, I entered a fish-and-chip shop and joined a queue. At the head of it was an elderly man with wild white hair and beard, wearing a grubby raincoat. I recognised William Golding. I mused about the odds against walking into a chippie and seeing a Nobel Laureate having fish and chips wrapped. He shuffled past me without recognition and I didn't say hello.

We'd met only a couple of times, shaking hands at large formal occasions in country houses. Sir William and Lady Ann had driven up in a long, sleek black car, to be instantly fawned on by Cornwall's minor gentry. I imagined that for the Goldings these invitations were ten-a-penny. They were rare for me, the gentry having quickly decided I wasn't 'one of them'. I smoked, and spilled wine and ash on their carpets, and my novels were indecent.

In June 1993, came a card inviting us to a party at the Golding residence. Denise didn't want to go; at heart still a working-class Cockney girl, she felt even more uneasy than I in grand surroundings, and among people most of whom she considered snobs. I drove off alone, taking the narrow winding road from Truro towards Falmouth, then in leafy Fal-side

Perranarworthal turning into the drive which led up to Tullimaar, a stately Georgian house. It was a beautiful June evening; the sun glinted off a couple of dozen parked cars.

Golding was greeting his guests in the hallway. We shook hands and I asked him, 'Are you writing a novel?' – that most infuriating question to a writer, since if you are, you don't want to talk about it, and if you're not, your spirits crash. But he was charitable, saying, with a sly smile, and tapping his nose, 'No. But I have an idea for one.' I said, 'That's good,' and moved past him.

Stately guests were sitting at card-tables, reminding me absurdly of working-class village whist-drives in my youth . . . Catcalls between tables: *'How'ee doin', Redvers?' 'Some 'andsome frock you got on 'night, Evie!'* . . . But these people at Tullimaar were delicately eating and drinking, between delicate arty remarks. I took a glass of wine from a waiter's tray, and found one or two people I knew. After a while I was pointed to another room, where other guests were lining up to be served carvings from a giant salmon, a giant ham. While eating I was introduced to Judy Carver, the Goldings' daughter, who had driven from her home in Bristol. A friendly woman, she showed me a plaque stating that General Eisenhower had stayed at Tullimaar while planning D-Day; then took me upstairs to show me where Eisenhower had slept; and a bullet-hole in a wall, caused by some drunk and trigger-happy American service-man, or maybe a would-be assassin – I don't remember which.

We went back down the broad stairs to the crowds – who were suddenly rushing for their coats and vanishing. It was as if another shot had been fired, announcing 'Our revels now are ended.' I looked at my watch. Ten o'clock! I couldn't believe it. I only get started at ten o'clock. I guess everyone thought, they're in their eighties, they like an early night, so we must go. In no time, the house was empty, apart from caterers clearing up, the Golding family, and me.

Judy said, 'Come into the parlour and we'll have another drink.'

Her brother David was there, sitting at the table. A gentle, utterly silent man. Ann Golding came in, regally elegant. Judy vanished and returned with a few bottles of red wine from the cellar. I opened one and we drank and chatted. I was gazing at portraits of William and Ann, each side the high wide window. 'A beautiful portrait of you,' I said; and she blushed. 'I was beautiful once,' she replied, looking wistful. I asked if she had any youthful photos she could show me. She went out and came back with an album, and showed me pictures of herself. 'Yes, you were a stunning girl.'

William Golding entered, and stopped short. 'You're showing him those photos!' he said angrily; and she seemed to wince. I said I'd asked her to show them to me, and she was beautiful; and his face softened as he sat down at the table. But then, noticing the wine bottles, barked at Judy, 'You've brought up my best wine!'

She murmured reprovingly, 'Oh, dad!' His face softened again, he poured himself a glass and relaxed. I asked them about their earlier lives; and my questions gradually ushered in an intimate, though veiled, father-daughter discussion across the table. When it turned to silence Golding stretched his hand to hers, and said, 'I do love you, you know.'

She gazed intently at him. 'I know you do.'

Time passed, in a blur of wine and talk. He said they'd moved to Cornwall – where he'd been born – to escape the crowds, but now people felt too intimidated to invite them out. 'I'm lonely.'

It surprised me, but also struck a chord. Denise and I had given up on hosting parties thinking guests meant it when they gushed 'You must come to us sometime'. Now here was the Nobel Laureate saying, 'I'm lonely.'

'So would you like to meet at a pub one evening?' I asked.

'Yes, I would.' He tore off a scrap of envelope and scribbled down his ex directory phone number for me.

Suddenly he gazed at his wife's portrait, then the window, the twilight beyond, and said, 'This *is* a beautiful house, isn't it?' It seemed like a moment of illumination, of grace.

I drank a lot, as did he. The window darkened. Ann stood up and said she was off to bed. As she passed him he took her hand, and said he would be up soon. I didn't take the hint; I started to sing, as I often do when I'm drunk and relaxed. I remember warbling the Beatles' 'Yesterday'. There were uneasy smiles, and I realised it was time to leave. One o'clock. I staggered out to my car, and saw them standing outside waving as I drove erratically away, seeing double. Two sets of cats-eyes.

The next evening I went to the opening of an art exhibition in Falmouth. A friend who'd been at the party greeted me: 'Such a shock about poor old Bill.' Golding had died at around 1.30 a.m., while getting ready for bed, of a massive heart attack.

I thought, My God, I've killed him! keeping him up too late and causing him to drink too much . . . I wrote to his daughter, commiserating with her and expressing those fears. She wrote back saying he had been suffering from severe heart problems and so his death was inevitable; and how better to die, than after seeing all his family and friends, on a beautiful midsummer evening?

Whatever images he held in his head for his next novel died with him. I still have his phone number, the last thing he wrote.

The Pen and the Ashtray

I've been thinking of an uncanny experience I had three or four years ago. A friend who claims to have psychic powers had swung her pendulum in my living room, hoping to contact Denise for me. The experiment had been inconclusive,

35

disappointing me. But when, at the end of the evening, I went upstairs to my study, I saw that my pen was resting on my ashtray, like an old-fashioned pen laid in an inkwell. It's something I would never do.

It seemed like her little joke. She knew how smoking and writing go together for me, and how my pen was inspired by her. Now I think she may have been hinting that I should record the nocturnal relationship, the secret trysts, we've had since her death. I wasn't able to write at the time. Could she have been saying, 'Write about us! You always did – though you'd call yourself Chartsky or Fartsky or something, and I'd be Masha or Natasha.'

In any case, it seems like something I should do. And this seems the right time to do it; she and *The White Hotel* are so bound up together.

Our very first encounter, after several weeks of being parted, was in a restaurant. There was that slightly nauseous, tremulous feeling, seeing again the woman who means so much to me. The restaurant seemed on the point of closing, the cutlery, glasses and tablecloths being cleared; but the waiters pushed two tables together in a corner for us. To my surprise and chagrin, another man came in and joined us. Handsome, suave guy. She introduced him as Max. I could sense, from the way they caught each other's eyes across the table, there had been intimacy between them, and I was stricken with jealousy. Just by looking across at someone, as she drew her Rothman from her sweet lipsticked mouth with her slender, erotic fingers, her eyelashes slightly lowered, she could rouse irresistible desire.

Denise excused herself to go to the toilet, and Max soon followed her. I was left alone, trying to read the menu, which was difficult as the lights had been dimmed. They were gone a long time. I could stand it no longer. I went to the stairway leading down to the toilets, and clattered down two flights.

Then I heard her call 'Don' from above. I looked up the stairs, and there she stood. She walked down to me.

'You must be kind to him,' she said; 'he's not well.'

Kind to *him*! How skilfully she can turn the tables, making me appear to be in the wrong. I noticed only now that her short jet-black hair had greyed, and had been styled into an old-fashioned perm. Her dress was old-fashioned too, and shapeless, stretched over her fat middle-aged stomach. Noticing my look, she said sadly, 'Sometimes I think it's hardly worth getting up in the morning. I've let myself go.'

'Yes, you have!' I said cruelly. So often, in the past, she'd make some self-critical remark, like 'This skirt makes me look fat', wanting me to contradict her, and I always did. But this time I felt angry, and wanted to punish her for letting herself go.

Pennies from a Blue Velvet Heaven

Besides replacing Bertolucci with David Lynch, Geisler and Roberdeau replaced their screenwriter. Out was Chuck Mee, after he'd written four drafts; in was Dennis Potter. It seemed like a glittering marriage: both gifted with original, bizarre, somewhat dark vision; mavericks from unfashionable places – Lynch from Missoula, Montana; Potter from the isolated, in-bred coal mining district of the Forest of Dean, on the borders of England and Wales. A marriage of *Eraserhead* and *Blue Velvet* with *Pennies from Heaven* and *The Singing Detective*.

There was also a remarkable series of synchronicities linking Dennis Potter and me. We were born in the same year, 1935, in working-class, mining communities. His father was a coal miner; the male members of my family had been tin miners, or craftsmen working in the mines. By the time I was born almost all the tin mines were dead, but all around my native village, Carnkie, near Redruth, were their evocative ruins. There were still stamps pounding, in tune with my heart, serving the one mine still working then. Dennis and I were selected at eleven to go to grammar schools, which gave us a chance to proceed to university – at a time when few working-class boys and even fewer girls did.

Before we could go to university, we had to do national service. He and I were both picked out to take a Russian course, and part of our time on it we spent at the Joint Services School for Linguists in Bodmin, Cornwall. (Fortunate for me, just thirty miles from my home; less so for him. But for both of us a damn sight better than fighting in Korea.) After the two years, we both took up a place at New College, Oxford. Since I was reading English and he History, our paths didn't cross; I was shy and studious, he threw himself into the Oxford Union, the Labour Club, Isis (the student magazine) and dramatic societies. I first saw him when watching a performance of Pirandello's *Man, Beast and Virtue*, in New College Gardens, during my last summer there. I remember nothing of the play or performance, except Dennis Potter's energy and red hair, flashing across the stage.

Twenty years later I wrote most of *The White Hotel* in a graduate building close to New College Gardens, and often turned the new work over in my mind as I strolled in the gardens where I'd seen Potter act. As editor of Isis in 1958, he may well have been responsible for my first publication, a short story which appeared, to my surprise and pleasure, in that magazine. I bought the magazine at the Oxford station bookstall as I left for the last time in my undergraduate years; flicked the pages – and there was my story, with a pen-and-ink illustration. It was a story set in my mining village, about an intelligent working-class boy beginning to explore sexual desire, and the theme could well have appealed to Potter.

When Geisler and Roberdeau persuaded him to take on the screenplay, he was living in Ross on Wye, not far from his childhood landscape. I was then still living in Hereford, only thirteen miles from him. I asked 'the boys' for his address, and wrote to him. I mentioned the extraordinary similarities and synchronicities in our lives, culminating in his screenplay of my novel, and how strange it was we had never met. I suggested we get together over a drink.

He replied, politely and coolly, that he thought meetings should happen by chance, not arrangement.

I don't know if he was concerned that I might try to influence the way he was approaching my book, or if the crippling psoriasis from which he suffered made him loath to be in company. Whatever the reason, we never met.

I know he was excited to be working with Lynch on *The White Hotel*. Geisler recalled the first face-to-face encounter between the two men, in the autumn of 1990 . . . A day of Biblical rain in New York . . . a winey dinner . . . On parting, Potter's face streamed with tears as his contorted, arthritic hands grasped Lynch's lapels. If they didn't screw it up, he said, if they saw it through to the end, this would be the work they would both be remembered by. 'This movie will be the *Madame Bovary* of our time.'

I *almost* met probably the most beautiful of all the beautiful actresses who have not played in *The White Hotel*: Isabella Rossellini. She was Lynch's girlfriend, and he wanted her as the lead. It seemed perfect – she with her European back-ground and culture. On one of the three or four trips I made to New York at Geisler and Roberdeau's invitation, I heard she was going to be flying in from Los Angeles. I asked the boys if we could have dinner with her; only it turned out she was arriving a day after my flight home. It would have been an experience to have sat at a table with 'one of the hundred most beautiful people in the world' (*People* magazine). I fantasised that she would be taken with me, my distinguished if unorthodox good looks, my Cornish accent smoothed – but not too much – by Oxford . . . She would be phoning me transatlantic, saying 'I must see you again. I'm going to Venice for the Festival; can you fly there and meet me? Come for a weekend. I have an apartment overlooking the Grand Canal. There are so many things about Lisa I want to talk to you about, Don . . . '

I did meet, slightly earlier, another star who I knew was being considered for the role; or rather, was being begged to take it on. It was a chance meeting – Dennis Potter would have approved. Returning to my New York hotel one day, I shared an elevator with an attractive woman wearing sunglasses. When she stepped out I thought: 'Jesus, that was Meryl Streep!' Dizzily I went up and down in the elevator three times, hoping somehow to find her again, and by miracle I did, since she almost at once came down again. I ran after her in the lobby. Still at heart a working-class boy from Cornwall, for whom 'the pictures' spelt magic, I was in awe. I called to her, 'Excuse me!' She turned round. 'Are you who I think you are?' She said yes, no doubt wondering who this annoying creep was. I introduced myself. She said, 'Oh my! I have your book by my bed!' I mumbled a few words about admiring her acting, then she went out and I returned to my room with trembling heart.

I later left her a card at the front desk, saying if she had time to meet for a drink . . . She didn't respond. But I treasure her radiant smile as, at cocktail hour, she swept in a dazzling gown through the hotel lounge towards the exit and recognised me. People all around looked at me, thinking – I hoped – 'Gee, he knows Meryl Streep! Wonder who he is!'

If Meryl finished reading my novel I don't know. If she conceived an imaginary picture with herself as Lisa, it didn't happen. Potter worked on his side of the great collaborative effort to create the *Madame Bovary* of our time. An admirer of his TV dramas, I eagerly awaited his screenplay.

Anger

I began to cherish the night-encounters with Denise. They haunted my mind after, like poignant images of a movie one has watched – far more potent than images from one's daily existence. I don't know what happened to Max; I never saw him again.

The next time Denise and I met, she had all her fire back. She was pursuing me around a bleak, huge, deserted hospital. This was undeniably a thriller movie. My heart raced, keeping just ahead of her. She was crippled and hobbling from her illness, but I still couldn't escape from her rage. It was as though I had weights on my feet, or had been maimed like Oedipus. I ran down empty corridors, through empty wards, and would think I'd escaped – only to find she'd taken a short-cut and was waiting around a corner for me, her face contorted.

She shouted that she'd put me on the doctors' duty roster, to take five per cent of the cancer patients. So now, as well as fleeing from her, I had nurses leaping out, saying, 'Dr Thomas, could you please take a look at . . . ' And worse, I was developing cancer myself; felt nausea, and had to run into a toilet cubicle to vomit.

She was waiting for me outside; said with a malign smile, 'That's just the start. You haven't felt anything yet, sunshine!' She always called me sunshine when she felt I was anything but.

We recovered from that violent episode, as we always did, and went to Albania. Not the most peaceful place, and once again we were in trouble – both of us this time. We were on the run from certain death if we were caught. Once, when people were searching for us, she made me bend down under a window, and kiss. She kissed so seductively. They would think we were harmless lovers.

'No, they've spotted us.' We had to race away. Only to be cornered by a real villain. He loomed over us, mouth twisted evilly, a knife in hand. She squatted, rocking back on her heels, gazing at him; then pulled up her skirt around her waist, and tugged her panties aside from her cunt. There was that mixture of pink flesh, hair and moistness goading him, between her plump white thighs and black fishnet stockings. He was spellbound, as I so often had been. His stare veered between her mocking, goading eyes and her mocking, goading, crystal-clear cunt. He went into a trance. 'Quick!' she said, getting slowly to her feet; then we raced away. He just stood there, his eyes glazed.

A Spring of Holly

Geisler and Roberdeau were an inseparable couple. Of course I only saw them now and again; but one just knew they never separated. They worked together and lived together, in Greenwich Village, New York. They were not lovers, Bobby told me much later; John was straight; but he had given up all thought of a marriage and children for this partnership with Bobby. They talked in a kind of operatic duet, one taking over from the other:

'Have you seen (*some movie by the latest director*) , Don?'

'Not yet.'

'When we first saw it, John and I were just . . . '

'Overwhelmed,' John would interrupt.

'Overwhelmed! We went for a meal afterwards, and neither John nor I spoke for about an hour . . . '

' – We were just completely shattered by it.'

' – And then John said to me, Are you thinking what I'm thinking? And I said, I think so! *The White Hotel*!'

John would chortle like a teenager, and say, 'He'll be just perfect for it, Don!'

'And he'll give the fantasy scenes the kind of – '

' – Innocence.'

' – Innocent or at least half-unconscious or limpidly youthful sensuality that it demands!'

And within two more hours they had personally delivered a copy of my novel to the director, with a bound copy of the latest screenplay, and within two days he had called back, 'Count me in!' I, my agent Andrew Hewson and his wife and agency partner Margaret, were swept away by their enthusiasm. And touched by their thoughtfulness. Every Christmas an Express Parcel service would deliver to my home a package, six foot tall and a foot square. Opening its complicated wrappings we would find – a branch of holly. I've no doubt Andrew and Margaret received one too.

And probably all the artists they had contracted to work with on the movie.

For sure, also, Terry Malick, with whom they had developed a deeper personal and creative relationship than I knew at the time.

So much went awry later, but I felt their warm friendship, their love for my novel, and their idealistic desire to make a great movie out of it. Now, in 1990, with Lynch and Potter on board, it looked within sight.

Potter's first draft screenplay arrived from them, with a request to read it and comment.

Clap Hands, here Comes Charlie

I know well, from translating Russian poetry, that often a translation has to be unfaithful to the letter in order to be true in the spirit. Nevertheless, it was a shock to find, almost immediately in the Potter script, an order over a loudspeaker calling for all Yids in Kiev to listen to a bulletin of the German High Command.

In my novel, the shock of Nazism comes as a brutal intrusion into the high culture of Europe, as represented by Freud's compassionate humanism and the world of opera. I did not intend a book about the Holocaust, but about the journey of a soul – Lisa's – in the first half of the twentieth century. I had tried to symbolise this by starting almost all the sections with a train journey. I couldn't see the point of bringing Babi Yar into the forefront.

A few lines later comes a circus *Big Top*, and music. Not the opening chords of *Don Giovanni*, which Geisler had dreamed of for so long, but 'the hot and sweet yet heart-breakingly innocent "Gloriana" as recorded by *Waring's Pennsylvanians, New York*, 1928 . . .' As the 'translucent and heavenly' *Big Top* fills the screen, the *vocal* begins:

> Singer (over)
> Glor–i–an–a
> Bu–do–do–do–dah–
> Look at that baby there –

Then, inside the tent, a gaudy circus band, with a singer lip-syncing . . .

> Blue eyes and golden hair
> Lovely! Gorgeous!
> That's Glor–i–an–a
> Ain't she the image of
> Someone you'd care to love
> O-O! So–So! Thay's Glor–i–an–a!

We are in Potter's own dream world, the world of sheet music, romantic songs of the twenties and thirties, a 'heart-breakingly innocent' world in his imagination. In the Big Top, Lisa, my opera singer, is swinging on the high wire, and Victor, the opera star from Kiev who becomes her second husband, is now a clown.

Big Dreams

I have an emotional sympathy with Dennis Potter's vision of a sheet music paradise. I still have in a music stool – which hardly anyone ever sits on – in front of a tinny old piano which almost no one ever plays – tattered sheet music belonging to my parents. Mostly with my father's name, H. R. Thomas, inscribed on the front. I can still hear their voices singing the romantic ballads, fifty and more years ago.

Yes, I hum the old songs in harmony with Potter, and feel stirred to the depths of me. Only Bu–do–do–do–dah didn't seem to be *The White Hotel.*

Moments later in the script, the circus performers are a mass of still, bloodied bodies; the tent is filled with Nazi soldiers who chant 'Juden! Juden! Juden!'

A recurrent melody in the Dennis Potter screenplay is 'Clap Hands here Comes Charlie', 'the great international hit'. We first hear it, played on a barrel organ, through the open window of a psychoanalyst's 'stuffily German' room. Lisa's analyst is not Freud, in the Vienna of 1919, but Probst, in Berlin 1928. He appears in only a few short scenes. I was dismayed to find Freud dismissed and the time scale of the novel so reduced. Bertolucci, apparently, had wanted too much Freud, now Potter didn't want any.

Lisa's sexual fantasy of the white hotel evoked some brilliant Potteresque imagery; but was it enough to make this *The White Hotel?* Without Freud, without opera, without the slow, relentless procession of history following the First World War? I conveyed my misgivings to Geisler.

'Well, Don,' came his reply, 'Lynch didn't feel he could handle European high art and culture.'

So much for *Madame Bovary,* I thought.

He thanked me for some incidental notes, which would be helpful to Dennis. They were going with this screenplay, basically; they thought it could work very well. It was all systems go. Lynch was going to join Bobby and John in Paris on New Year's Eve, 1990, to sign his contract and celebrate the beginning of a great venture.

'Clap hands here comes Charlie.'

A New Coat

After our nocturnal adventure in Albania, Denise and I settled back into life in Hereford. Then one night she said to me, 'I'm going with Cath and Roger to Bangor.' There was pain and threat in her eyes as she added, 'We may never see each other again.'

I had that old panicky feeling. I knew why she was threatening this: the resentment because I still lived with Maureen. Our close friends Cath and Roger were Welsh, so I could understand why they might be going to Bangor, in North Wales. I had driven through the dour grey-skied town once, when visiting a Welsh girlfriend – the only time I, rather than Denise, had tried to end an impossible situation by leaving her.

I looked at her, so handsome and strong. I made a sudden decision. 'I'll leave Maureen, you can move in with me. And then we'll go to Cornwall.'

'If you're sure . . . ' She looked pleased. She ruffled up her skirt to re-fasten a suspender which had sprung loose: as a kind of reward to me. That ample thigh, that black suspender, those nimble fingers I never tired of seeing in this familiar act . . . First seen through my mother or sister dressing, and in the village Sunday School socials . . . 'I'm sure.' Though immediately I felt a slight pang at the future women, the brief flings, I'd be giving up. But the essential thing was not to lose Denise. It would be unbearable.

'I'll have to give Maureen quite a lot; we'll have to buy a small house. Unless Cath and Roger move in with us.' That seemed a nice idea. I like loosening the tight knot of coupledom.

We went to a party. I danced with a plump middle-aged

woman, running my hands over her waist and ass. She was married and respectable, but became turned-on by the dance and my hands. She murmured, 'I could do with a quickie. How about coming outside, to help me get my car started?' I wanted to; but Denise was there, talking to some others. I said I'd better not. Then Denise started abusing me coarsely. 'Cunt! Prick-face! You're a fucking asshole!' The other guests fell silent, then gradually melted away, embarrassed. I said to her, 'How dare you shout at me like that!'

She said, her green eyes twinkling, 'Oh, they know we always make up – and how good that is!'

She'd always been fond of saying the word *cunt*. She would shock Ross's teenage friends by using it; and when she was being sewn up after he was born, she shocked the doctor by saying, 'God, what a job! staring up women's cunts all the time!' I loved that brazenness in her. Cunt is an expressively dark, dynamic word, when used accurately; I can tell if I'm going to like a woman by whether she loves or loathes the word. Denise loved it.

Another time we met at 'St Martin's Villa', the house in Carnkie where I was born and where I have my first memory – of fighting for breath at six months during an attack of whooping cough. My mother held me in her arms, my aunt Cecie gazed at me, anxious. There was a misty light at the window, the kitchen window that looks out (as I discovered later) at green fields shading to brown, the ruined mine-stacks and engine houses, then rising to bouldered, primeval Carn Brea. Now I was here again, sixty five years on, with Denise. She was warm and loving; but became sulky when we realised all my family was in the house too. 'I suppose I'll have to hide from them,' she said. She'd spent too many years skulking with me in the shadows.

'I don't see why you should do that.' Though I felt perhaps she was right.

She was looking pretty well considering she was terminally ill. I wondered if the doctors had made a mistake. I thought, great, I can look after her and really love her! She was putting on a new coat. She said in a cheerful voice, 'The doctors have said I can wear it out at least once.'

Once didn't sound very optimistic to me. Why was she cheerful? Maybe she heard it as 'wear it till it's threadbare'. A good coat will last twenty or more years before you wear it out.

An Imaginary Degas

I can imagine the scene at the Ritz Hotel in Paris on New Year's Eve, 1990. For this special occasion even Bobby Geisler, normally Bohemian in dress, occasionally clownlike, is in a smart suit and tie. Possibly even a tuxedo. They would be enjoying the Gallic revelry around them in the restaurant. They would be sipping aperitifs, and Dom Perignon would be on ice. Two neatly-bound copies of David Lynch's contract would rest on the wide white tablecloth. There would also be, probably, a gift for David to mark the solemn occasion. Perhaps it's a limited edition print by Degas of a high-wire artiste, caught in mid-flight. At any rate, something exquisite and appropriate. I treasure still the lovely glass swan they sent to me, picking up an image in the book.

They have been searching for a gift all afternoon, and at last found this beautiful print on the Left Bank. 'Let's get it for David,' Geisler would have said.

'It's lovely – and it's expensive. Can we afford it?'

'No, but what the hell? This is a special occasion. This is where our dream becomes reality.'

'You're right.'

So the gift, perfectly wrapped by a charming gallery assistant, will be resting on David's table-setting opposite them. They wait for him to arrive from Los Angeles. They wish Dennis could have come too. They will call him, they agree, just at midnight. 'Dennis!' Bobby would chortle. 'Happy New Year! And we have some wonderful news for you: John and I are here at the Ritz having dinner with David; and we have just signed his contract! I'll pass the phone to him . . . '

John Roberdeau glances at his watch. 'David should be landing about now.'

A waiter comes up to their table, bows obsequiously, and says there is a phone call for Monsieur Geisler. 'That'll be him,' Geisler says, rising and following the waiter out to the lobby. He picks up the ornate telephone. 'Hi!'

'Bobby.'

'David! Are you at Charles de Gaulle?'

A pause. Then, 'No, in California. Bobby, Isabella and I have broken up.'

'Oh, Jeez, I'm so sorry!'

'I can't make this movie without her.'

'Oh!'

'I'm sorry.' And the phone clicks off.

That's how I imagine it, from a heartbroken sentence or two from Bobby. David Lynch might have a different story. In any case, the Lynch-Potter *White Hotel* would remain an imaginary picture.

Three years later, Dennis Potter died of pancreatic cancer, a week after his wife died of breast cancer. For me, their dying almost simultaneously in their separate agonies is one of the saddest stories in the whole *White Hotel* saga. They endured, in their private world, their own holocaust.

Salon Kitty

Denise and I were separated again. She was working in a Berlin brothel. I recognised it as the brothel in the film *Salon Kitty*, full of uniforms – the men in their S.S. gear and the girls in their own S.S. uniform of black swastika-like Stockings and Suspenders. The girls were secretly helping the Allies. Denise was protecting one of the whores; it involved her in having to sleep with one or two men.

Walking with her through a Berlin street I said, 'I hate you doing this, you know that, don't you?' – wanting to show I still had strong feelings for her.

'Yes,' she said, which encouraged me. I wanted to ask her if she still loved me; but held back, fearing it was too soon, that she might say No.

'Whenever we renew our love it seems like a renewal of hate,' she said sadly.

I was hurt; why couldn't she see the obvious, that love-hate is the most intense love? I wanted to say, 'You just don't know how choked up with love for you I am,' but I was too choked up to say it.

Not so long after I managed to be with her as she was going into labour. Her father was present too. She said, 'You must ring my mother, Don.'

'There's no hurry; labour takes a long time.'

'I know that, you fool! But she doesn't even know I'm pregnant, let alone that I'm going to have an abortion.'

I said tenderly, 'We can keep it if you want'; but she said sadly, 'No.'

She'd been forced to give up a baby for adoption at twenty two; had another aborted at the end of a brief affair when she was trying to escape her painful relationship with me; we had a healthy child, Ross; then at forty another, Richard, was still-born. She endured too much. All that conceivably can happen to a woman who's with child had happened to her. If anyone had experienced the full spectrum of the white hotel, it was she.

TWO

Phoning the Dead

Licking Wounds

After David Lynch's withdrawal from the movie project in 1990, Geisler and Roberdeau seemed to go into a retreat for several years. I pictured them licking their wounds. Occasionally they would emerge briefly: to tell me, for example, that Hector Babenco was being considered as director. They sent a video of *Kiss of the Spider Woman*. And invariably there was the sprig of holly at Christmas.

In reality they were not so much licking their wounds as licking another artist's ego; and thereby sowing trouble for themselves and for me. I knew nothing of their activities, other than what they chose to tell me. I wasn't *au fait* with the cultural life of Hollywood – or anywhere else for that matter. I was living quietly and writing quietly in Cornwall. *Flying in to Love* came out in 1992, along with a *New & Selected Poems*, *The Puberty Tree*; *Pictures at an Exhibition*, in '93; *Eating Pavlova* in '94; *Lady with a Laptop* in '96. They mostly had good reviews, but none of them sold very well. Then Robert Weil, of St Martin's Press, New York, invited me to write a biography of Alexander Solzhenitsyn. I cringed at the thought of it – all that research, all that non-fictional writing; but we needed the money. I deeply admired Solzhenitsyn, and felt that his life 'contained' almost the entire Russian twentieth century. That, I hoped, could provide a wider, richer theme than one writer's life. I would write about the great and heroic poets and novelists, in that carnivorous epoch. So I accepted, and plunged into research that was deeply inimical to me.

My writing, throughout the decade, was taking place against dark events in our family life. We had a swimming pool built – hoping it would encourage Ross to find some friends in his new life in Cornwall; and later unmade the pool – hoping that would diminish the pain of recall of a day of overwhelming tragedy. It's not something I can write about. Ross, after his trauma of plunging into the murky pool to find a missing toddler – my daughter Caitlin's first son Alex – developed post-viral fatigue syndrome, and had scarcely any secondary education. My little grandson died two years after the pool accident. Then, soon after I began the Solzhenitsyn, came the diagnosis of Denise's cancer. As I struggled with the biography she struggled to stay alive and all three of us struggled to survive.

As Denise's end drew near, we thanked God for that mysterious new entity, the internet; because Ross 'met' a Canadian woman, through something mysterious called a 'chat-room' – a Christian chat-room; went to Toronto for a visit with her, and very quickly they fell in love. I managed to arrange for him to start a journalism course there, at Humber College, Toronto, for whom I undertook correspondence courses and an annual writing workshop. I have a cherished photo of mother and son together, Denise somehow managing to smile, the day he left for Toronto. An agonising parting, for she was declining quite quickly. Driving back from the railway station, I remember sobbing loudly in tune with my car-horn blaring, for it had decided to sound continuously.

Grief-stricken, yet also in love, Ross was able to start a new life. I had to send for him a few weeks later to come and say goodbye to his mother in a St Austell hospice. He stayed a week. He told me that as the train from Truro to London stopped at St Austell, the next town up the line, he was sobbing loudly, to the consternation of the other passengers, and it took all his willpower not to jump off. I don't know how he found the courage not to. For me, it was hard spending some of each day with Denise, watching her fade, but it would have been even harder not to have been with her. A small part of me wanted the agony to end, so I could actually start the process of grieving; the greater part of me wanted her to live on and on, even if it meant my spending the rest of my life visiting her in the hospice. She still looked very beautiful; indeed, never more so.

I was there to light her very last Rothman, and to take it unfinished from her fingers as the morphine drip kicked in. She had wondered if, when the moment came, she would want to die alone or try to wait for me to visit. Our friends Cath and Roger from Hereford, Ross's godparents, were staying with me. We'd left her in a coma in the late afternoon, and came back in the evening. There was a huge full moon ahead of the car, and the sky was dramatic, stormy. I felt it as a portent. Denise was struggling for breath as Cath and I rushed in. She had waited for us. I caught hold of her hand and said, 'Denise, we love you. I love you, Ross loves you. God loves you. You have been good to children and animals. And all shall be well, and all manner of things shall be well.' She stopped breathing and her eyes opened.

There, I've written about it. A little. Enough.

So really, in these years – between the pool tragedy and Denise's illness – I didn't give a fig what Geisler and Roberdeau were up to. After Potter's death in 1994, they invited me to New York for a reading performance of his screenplay. It took place at the Lincoln Center, and as always no expense was spared. The actors included Rebecca De Mornay, Brian Cox and Len Cariou; staging by Anne Bogart, sound score by Hans Peter Kuhn; Lauren Flanigan singing and the Hudson Shad recreating the period music. Most of these names meant nothing to me, but I knew they were distinguished people because Bobby caressed their names. After the performance, there was dinner al fresco for three hundred guests.

I ended the evening lounging in Rebecca De Mornay's hotel

bedroom, talking and drinking her minibar dry. She was trying to get over Leonard Cohen. I'd had no idea they'd been together. Not that Leonard Cohen meant much to me. I overstayed my welcome and wrote her a note of apology in the morning, before leaving to catch my flight home.

The Lincoln Center event was a touching tribute to Potter from the producers; and also no doubt they hoped to revive interest in the project. Then they told me they were taking time-out from *The White Hotel* for a while: they'd asked Terrence Malick again if he'd direct it; he'd again declined but said he was prepared to direct an adaptation of James Jones' World War Two novel *The Thin Red Line*. I felt a little peeved; but I could understand their decision. I knew how much Malick's work meant to them. Well, no, I didn't understand the extent of it. If I had happened to read the December '98 issue of *Vanity Fair* magazine, I would have understood it. It would have been an eye-opener. But I wasn't reading glossy magazines then; I was grieving, struggling with loneliness, oppressed by the early fall of darkness, and passing some of the dark hours by trying to get to grips with internet.

A Sharp Edge

Another night Denise and I met in the pub at Piece, a hamlet five minutes walk from Carnkie. My grand parents had once kept the little shop near the pub, in the busy mining days. Indeed, back in the nineteenth century, three of my four sets of grandparents lived in neighbouring miners' cottages there– Thomases, Moyles, Jeffreys. Though many in all families were in mines overseas. Butte City and Johannesburg were nearer than Plymouth, Devon. Now, Piece isn't even a hamlet, just a pub.

Once, the Countryman would have been full of tin miners, cracking jokes, discussing rugby, swearing, then singing

Methodist hymns in perfect drunken harmony. Denise and I touched hands. I was upset, and told her why. Three women with whom I'd had affairs had committed suicide. One, called Julie, had just walked calmly into the sea. The other drinkers in the pub became curious, listening in to our conversation. They stood up and gathered round us, silent. We started to talk loudly about even more scandalous things than suicides and affairs – fictionalising, to tease our listeners.

Later we strolled down to Carnkie, passing the chapel and 'St Martin's Villa', the house of my birth. In the square outside the chapel, my auntie Susan-Jane one night took off all her clothes, and danced. She was taken 'up Bodmin', to the lunatic asylum. Denise said she could hear people whispering behind the hedges: the voices sounded American, and threatening. She began attacking me for involving her in this. She was suddenly angry and bitter. I thought, if she weren't so bitter so often, I wouldn't have been unfaithful to her.

'We can go somewhere else, live somewhere else,' I said. 'No more infidelities, Denise! These suicides are a lesson to me. We'll start afresh.'

We lay down in a field and I tried gently to finger fuck her. Just as gently she said I had a sharp nail. I felt guilty that I'd left a sharp edge.

An Unlucky War

For most of the 90s, apart from the lavish tribute to Potter at the Lincoln Center, Geisler and Roberdeau went missing from my life. There would always be the sprig of holly at Christmas, as if to remind me they were still on the planet. I was absorbed in writing, and in the stresses and tragedies of private life. It didn't, and doesn't, matter if *The White Hotel* is never made into a film. It was only the spasmodic bursts of enthusiasm and activity from Geisler and Roberdeau which kept exciting me momentarily, when I'd think, Hey, this might get made after all! And that would be a pretty interesting experience! It would be nice for my family too, to be able to swank it up at first night in London or New York.

The producers burst back in, in 1997. 'Hi, Don, it's Bobby here – howya doin'? . . . We have some great news – we have a director for *The White Hotel* who John and I think will make an amazing movie . . . ' It was the Sarajevo-born Emir Kusturica. I'd never heard of him. 'Emir has such *macho* energy, Don! And such passion for the cinema! He's a whirlwind – you'll love him!' And the beauty of it was, they could film it in Yugo-slavia; they could build the white hotel set on a lake; and they could take their pick of the whole Yugoslavian army for extras.

I asked about the script: would they use Dennis Potter's? No, not exactly; Emir would work on it with his cousin, adapting Potter's. Maybe Freud could be brought back in, though not the opera.

When I met them for a brunch in New York, in February '98, during a short visit to launch my Solzhenitsyn biography, they were in an exuberant mood. All was going well. They hoped Juliette Binoche would play the lead; though Emir feared she was not sensual enough. They were sure they could persuade him she was. But if not, there were other big stars who would kill to play Lisa. Nicole Kidman, for instance. Towards the end of the year – a year which, for me, was the most painful of my life – 'the boys' were in London. My agent's wife and business partner, Margaret, a dashing and spirited Scottish woman, rang me and said, 'We had dinner with Bobby and John, and Kusturica and Juliette Binoche, last night.' I said, 'And they didn't think of inviting me?' She said, 'Andrew told them not to, because you're grieving for Denise.'

'That was very thoughtful of him,' I said, 'but I'd like to have been given the choice.'

A moment of hesitation. 'Yes, you should have been. Sorry.'

Geisler and Roberdeau had charmed them, as they had charmed me. They would have a lunch or dinner with Andrew on his regular professional trips to New York. We all thought they had simply had bad luck in their attempt to get the movie off the ground, especially with Lynch; they had fulfilled their contractual obligations, and we could hardly fault them for generosity and kind gestures. This time, everything looked good. I once again had a vision: of a white hotel springing up by magic beside a Serbian lake, with snowy mountains behind, and fir trees; and all those extras from their army scurrying around as waiters and ski-lift operators. Kidman or Binoche on a train, rising into the mountains, with the hand of Freud's son gliding up under her skirt, and his cigar smoke making her hair catch fire.

Then, in March 1999, NATO forces bombed Serbia.

Kusturica's son almost died when a bomb fell just forty yards from him in Belgrade.

Exit Emir, understandably enraged with the West, especially America. Instead of directing *The White Hotel*, he acted in a French Canadian film, *La Veuve de St Pierre* – with the 'unerotic' Juliette Binoche.

Grief

My agent's kindly-meant advice to 'the boys' not to invite me to London to have dinner with Kusturica and Binoche could not have been more mistaken. After Denise's death, and the final departure of Ross for Canada, I hated the autumn evenings drawing in, my isolation and grief increased by darkness outside.

On the day following the funeral I took the train to London. Duckworth, who had earlier commissioned me to write a novel (*Charlotte*) in their series Duckworth Literary Entertainments, was celebrating the firm's hundredth, or maybe thousandth, anniversary with a lavish party at the Grosvenor House Hotel.

I was, of course, totally not in the mood for lavish parties; but it was better than facing that first day alone, after my children and friends had gone. And I would be staying overnight with London-Russian friends who were warm-hearted and Slavonically hospitable. I wore, for only the second time in my life, a dinner jacket.

While leggy models dressed to look like swans, or maybe ducks, brought drinks around, I sat at a large table with strangers. I'm ill at ease at the best of times with London *chatterati*, and the conversations I had were meaningless. Then, late in the evening, I spotted John Bayley standing not far away, amid a cloud of literary folk; and beside him, his wife Iris Murdoch, wearing a drab, shapeless Oxfam-style frock. Bayley had been my stuttering and brilliant tutor at New College, Oxford. He had married Iris during my undergraduate years. I met her just once there. Having developed eye strain in my last year, I was given permission to type my Finals papers. I sat in lone and nervous splendour in the Warden's Lodge at New College, my battered portable typewriter – even more battered when I wrote *The White Hotel* on it twenty years later – before me. And on one occasion Iris sat with me, invigilating. Her eyes seemed kind and all-seeing. I met John a few times in later years, but Iris only once, when they generously came to do a reading at the modest College of Education in Hereford where I was a lecturer in English.

Now, when I approached John and he said, delightedly, 'Ah, my dear fellow!' he introduced me to Iris, with a chortle: 'Iris, it's T-t-typewriter Thomas!' Though for gone into the darkness of Alzheimer's, she seemed to understand. In any case she took hold of my arms, stared deeply into my eyes, and proceeded to engage me in conversation. She twittered like a sparrow; and anyone in a normal state of mind would have regarded what she was saying as gibberish; but I was not in a normal state of mind, and I mumbled a few words whenever she paused for a moment. I spoke of my grief, and Iris seemed to understand that too. We conversed mostly with our eyes. I sympathised with her sorrow, and she with mine. Then I went back to the articulate people with whom I couldn't communicate.

Iris died a few months later.

I grieved for Denise, and also studied my grieving. A lot of it, of course, was simple grief because I missed her. She had been intricately woven into my life for over thirty years. It was an amputation. But just as great a part of it was my grieving *on her behalf*, because she had lost so much of life, dying at 53. I hated it that she, so vivid, so intensely life-loving, had lost her life. It's a simple phrase, as in 'he lost his life in a car accident'; but it was so poignant, so total; it's not like losing a purse. Besides that, I felt deep remorse, for things done and things undone. And finally, I grieved for what Ross had lost; I didn't know how he could bear the loss of his mother. I felt for Denise's mother too, a spiky, unsociable and increasingly housebound widow who had come to live near her daughter, and who had no one else in her life. No, bereavement wasn't simple.

With a friend called Victoria I went for a short winter break to Madeira. In the Anglican church, at Sunday service, I sobbed throughout; and for the first and only time in my life, having been brought up a Methodist, I took Communion. 'I heartily repent . . . ' weeping all through it. I had much to repent.

I cried at least once a day for almost a year. I saw a grief counsellor, and she was a little help. I saw the old Anglican priest who had helped Denise in the hospice to – perhaps, sort of – come to terms with death; I recall him pressing his hands down on my head as he murmured a blessing. That comforted, for an hour. Above all, two women friends invited me to dinner once a week, for several months. The sense that they cared helped most of all.

I had suffered painful bereavements before, but one forgets. Now I pored over books about bereavement. Of all the sage advice, the most helpful was a passage which used a metaphor of wave-motion. I should expect, at first, the waves of grief to be monstrously high, with brief intermissions. Gradually, as after a storm, the waves would be mostly a little less high, and the intermissions a little longer. In time there would be mostly calm waves, but occasional surges as high as they had been at the beginning. This is how it turned out. Learning to expect this pattern helped me to cope with it.

And then there was a book I happened to pick up, God knows why: *The Last of England*, by Ted Walker. I knew him slightly. At the beginning of my career as a writer, I had sent some poems to a magazine called *Priapus*. Its editor, John Cotton, encouraged me, and published a few juvenile poems of mine. There were poems in *Priapus* by Ted Walker which had a distinctive and original voice, far in advance of mine.

Much later I invited him to read at Hereford College. He proved to be a burly, dark haired, affable man with a wonderful gift for anecdotes. Later still I met him at an event connected with Thomas Hardy. But I couldn't say I knew him. On reading *The Last of England*, though, I felt strongly drawn to him, and knew I wanted to get in touch.

His book related the long-drawn-out death, by cancer, of his wife of thirty two years. It was the same space of time I had known Denise. After his wife died, he went for a few months to Spain, a country which had fascinated him, as an escape from his memories. He described how, one evening, tormented by grief, he drove many miles to the nearest village to find a phone-booth. There he had pressed in the coins and dialled his home telephone number in Sussex. As the phone rang in his empty home, he dreamed that his wife would answer.

I could understand completely that mad drive through the darkness to a phone. And a call which a part of him was sure his dead wife would answer. I myself heard Denise's voice, three or four times, shouting up the stairs in her stentorian tones:

'Do-o-ON!' That the-poor-dog-needs-a-walk voice. I knew the state of mind in which his action was perfectly sensible.

He had re-married. There had been a couple, their best friends, and the husband in that relationship had died almost at the same time as Ted's wife. Now, widower and widow found comfort in each other's company; Ted had moved in with her, but it hadn't worked out. Then she had agreed to move into *his* home, in Chichester – if he was prepared to put in a new kitchen, as Ted's wife had long been asking for. He put the kitchen in; and I could feel his unspoken remorse that he hadn't done so earlier.

I had no idea where he was now, or what his life was like; *The Last of England* was several years old; but I knew I had to try to get in touch with him. Only he, a fellow poet, one who had lost his wife of thirty years to cancer, and who knew about guilt, would be able to talk to me in the right language. I wrote to him via the publisher, telling him what his book had meant to me.

About two weeks later I received a letter from him, with Spanish stamps on the envelope. I could have no idea, it said, what my letter had meant to him. He and Audrey, his second wife, had moved to Spain; they were happy, yet not a day went by without his remembering his first wife. He would be very happy to correspond with me, and would try to help. Probably the best way would be by fax. He did not have a fax machine at home, but there was a shop in the village which had one, and he visited it most days.

I faxed him back. And then we corresponded, every other day. We talked about grief, and new unions, and memory; remorse and self-forgiveness. I became reliant on his faxes, and I think he on mine. I gathered that they had moved to Spain because he couldn't bear Mrs Thatcher's England – whereas I had enjoyed her bracing radicalism; yet he had a feeling of being in exile.

After a month or so I received a fax in which he wrote: 'Audrey feels that through your faxes she knows you almost as well as I. And I feel that, from having been past acquaintances, we have now become fast friends. We would like to invite you to come for a visit . . . '

I accepted. We arranged it for February 1999. Denise had been dead four months. Ted wrote that they thought it best for me to stay, as other visitors to them did, at a very nice little guest-house in the village – since everyone needs periods of privacy. I agreed with him. A couple of days before I was due to fly to Alicante, the nearest airport, Ted rang me and said spring had come already; he had been in the garden naked to the waist. They were so looking forward to my visit. 'Smoke as much as you like, it's no problem!'

When I landed, they were an hour late arriving to pick me up, from having got the flight-time wrong; but it didn't matter, their greeting was full of warmth. It was about an hour's drive to their village in the hills. They dropped me at the little guest-house, and said they would collect me in a couple of hours to take me to their favourite restaurant. The guest-house, I found, was extremely spartan, and I was disconcerted to find there was no phone, except a private one to be used for emergencies. I wanted to be able to ring Victoria, who had helped me with the Solzhenitsyn and with whom I'd become involved. Someone whom I needed to help me get through this grief and loneliness, though of course her very presence in my life brought remorse and guilt – increasing the pain I needed her help to get through.

It had been a painful situation for her too, living hundreds of miles away and with, mostly, only phone contact. At one low point she had rung to say she was finishing; we shouldn't meet so long as Denise was alive. The shock to me was so overwhelming – I couldn't see how I could cope with Denise's dying without her emotional support – that I suffered an instant 'stroke' draining almost all the strength from my right hand. Psychosomatic, I guess. I begged, Victoria relented, and after a few weeks my hand became strong again.

The evening in the restaurant with the Walkers went well. I liked Audrey, a pleasant, homely woman. And Ted was clearly excited at my visit. We had all three suffered a similar loss; and that evening, back in my spartan guest-house bedroom, I started a poem – the first I had been able to write for a year or more – about there having been six of us sharing a meal together.

In the morning Audrey, not Ted as promised, came to pick me up and drive me to their home. She said Ted was a little unwell, but it was nothing to worry about. He had some heart problems, but the Spanish health service was wonderful. 'I want you to know,' she said, 'how thrilled he is that you've come; how important your visit is to him. Last night we stayed up talking for hours.' I said how important it was to me too; I owed Ted so much.

Their charming, very Spanish house, draped in bougan-villaea, was in a little enclave of immigrants, mostly German and English. Ted seemed fine, and proudly showed me round. The weather had turned, the temperature falling abruptly; it started to snow. We drove to the nearest seaside town and had lunch huddling against a chill, snowy wind in a seafront café. It reminded me of bleak days in Cornish resorts. I read them my poem; they were pleased with it. We were happy to eat quickly and get back to their warm house. The bitterly cold weather continued, and for the next three days we were cooped up in their small living room – when I was not freezing and bored in the unheated guest-house. I smoked as much as I liked, which is constantly. The weather was an unlucky accident; I knew it was difficult for all of us, not being able to get out into the open air, sitting on their patio, basking in early spring sunshine. We watched videos, and tried to find new things to say. Ted and I argued over the Falklands War. I had rejoiced with and for Margaret Thatcher; Ted – even more strongly than all but a handful of British writers and intellectuals – had prayed the Argentinians would win, so that Maggie would be forced to resign. He called the islands the Malvinas.

I argued forcefully, pointing out that the Argentinians had won democracy too as a result of our victory; but I cut it short, realising Ted wasn't pleased, and I was their guest. That was the only disagreement. He showed me some new poems he was working on, and told me about conflicts in his family. He had cut off contact with a brother and a son. And, of course, England. A man of decisive cut-offs.

The three days were a strain for all of us. I could see Ted was a few degrees cooler towards me than at first, though still friendly enough. I invited them to come and visit me in Cornwall. Audrey said she would like to, but didn't know if Ted could be dragged there. Ted said it would be best if we corresponded by letter in future, since faxing was expensive and they weren't well off. They asked one of their English neighbours to drive me to the airport.

Clearly my departure was a relief to all of us. Yet only, I thought, because it's intolerable for three people – one a guest and a constant smoker – to be in one room for almost the whole of three days. My affection and gratitude hadn't faltered. I rang them as soon as I got home. Ted answered, and seemed neither warm nor unfriendly. I asked them what they were doing, and he said they were catching up with the *Times* crosswords.

I thanked them again in a letter, saying how marvellously hospitable they had been, and that I knew the bad weather had made my visit a strain for them. I also said unwisely and tactlessly that – with future visitors in mind – they might like to know that the guest-house wasn't very comfortable in wintry conditions, though it would be charming in warmer weather.

A week or so later I received a card: 'Don, Thank you for

your Collins. Audrey and I have talked, and we've decided that we wish you well, but can do no more for you. This is therefore the end of our correspondence, and indeed of our friendship. Ted.'

I had to look up 'Collins' in the dictionary. An 'insincere thank you letter', the word originating in the Rev. Collins' famous letter in *Pride and Prejudice*. I felt terribly upset. I wrote back begging them to tell me how I had offended them, so that I could apologize. I'd probably smoked too much, not given them enough money to pay for a couple of international calls from their home; and of course I ought not to have criticised the guest-house. But they of all people, I wrote, should know that a bereaved person doesn't always behave impeccably. Ted must also surely know that this curt breaking off of friendship undid all the kindness of his faxes. I wrote three times, in similar vein; they didn't reply.

From being fast friends we had again become past acquaintances. I could only handle it as a piece of black comedy. I'd roar with laughter when showing the card to friends. Some of them thought I must have made a pass at Audrey. I assured them I hadn't.

I obsessed about the rejection; knew the card by heart. He could so easily, I felt – deciding I was not very congenial after all – have written a few friendly letters, at increasingly wide intervals, and turned our relationship gradually into an exchange of Christmas cards. Obviously he wanted to be as hurtful as possible; and that meant he had himself been badly hurt by me. Somehow.

Later, a book of his short stories was published in Britain. I wrote him a note of congratulations. He didn't acknowledge it. When he had written 'the end of our correspondence' he had meant it.

In March 2004, I read his obituary in the *Times*. I felt sad, and sent Audrey my condolences. Despite our rift, I wrote, I would always be grateful for Ted's faxes, and he had been a fine poet. I hoped she might respond, but she didn't. My feelings towards Ted now are mostly of sadness for him: sadness that, in some way I don't understand, I disappointed him.

The Kiss

We kissed. When Denise kissed you, putting all her flesh and spirit into it, it was unforgettable. But it had been so long since we had kissed that I'd forgotten it. Her open lips seemed to melt into yours; your head started to spin with the wonder of it; and you'd see, as you both withdrew for a second or two, her upper lip curled back a little, exposing her white teeth: expressing tenderness and a sense of pleasure in her mastery of this art, this art of kissing. I remember a few years before her death, when we fell in love all over again, we kissed and made love almost the whole of one night. The universe became our joined, melted mouths, and that divine aching pleasure where it was my cunt and her prick, as much as it was her cunt and my prick.

Tonight, sprawling on a sofa, we had not got further than the kissing. But I sensed she wanted to fuck. I worried I would not rise to the occasion, since I had masturbated before sleep. Yet with Denise in this seductive mood, who could fail to respond? I slid my hand under her bra and cupped her small breast. Then I stroked her neck and shoulders; I found she was quite bony there, and I thought this was the only sign of her illness. This was a different narrative, I thought, a different story; and perhaps in this one she needn't go on to die.

Of course these secret, nocturnal meetings were hard on the new live-in woman in my life. And Denise would very occasionally visit her old home and, as it were, leave her calling-card. Usually when Victoria was away or out. The pen in the ashtray, for instance. Another time, I returned to my study to work, after a few hours' absence, and was astonished to see a picture on my screen. It ought to have been blank, or showing the screen-saver; instead, there was a smiling woman flirtatiously holding her skirt up to her hips, revealing her black stocking tops and suspenders. She would know that would turn me on. I left the study again to go downstairs for something; and when I came to climb the stairs again our Cairn terrier, Tamsin, was at the top, not archly looking down at me as she commonly did, her head cocked sideways, but gazing to her right along the corridor towards my study, her tail wagging in surprise and pleasure.

Then there was a morning when I couldn't find my nail-scissors. Usually I leave them on a wide white window ledge in the en suite bathroom. They weren't there. I hunted high and low, in every room where I could conceivably have left them. Victoria was away, the house was empty. Returning to the en suite bathroom, I saw them at once on the window ledge – black scissors on white, unmissable. I had to smile. *Mischievous bitch!* . . .

Paris / New York

After NATO's war on Serbia put paid to their latest plans for the film, Geisler and Roberdeau seemed to withdraw again to lick their wounds – which of course were nothing like the wounds inflicted on Serbs and Albanians alike. I heard nothing from them for a couple of years. But an important date was coming up in July 2001. It would then be ten years since they had exercised their option on my novel, and the contract contained a standard clause reverting the rights to me, if principal photography hadn't begun within ten years. My agent, Andrew, kept sending them reminders that this deadline was coming up in a few months. No response came.

Then, out of the blue, we received an invitation from them

to spend a weekend in Paris in February, to discuss the future of the project. Andrew's wife Margaret, his partner in the small John Johnson Agency, was included in the invitation – a sign of the friendship that had been built up over the infertile but entertaining years. I was pleased she would be present, because she was vivacious and shrewd; and it couldn't do any harm to have the whole agency there to cast their professional eyes over any new contract that might be on offer.

I flew from Plymouth to Paris, on a little Jersey Airlines plane. No limo this time – a taxi to the Pont-Royal Hotel. The hotel too, when I entered the shabby, cupboard-size 'lobby', seemed remarkably down-market for Geisler and Roberdeau. Then I found it was the wrong hotel – the *Port* Royal. My French is not great; once, in a Montmartre restaurant, I waved at a waiter and demanded in a lordly way, proud of knowing the word for ashtray, '*Un fumier, s'il vous plaît*'. A dung-heap.

Eventually I reached the right hotel. The others were already there. Hugs and exclamations of pleasure all round. Over the first of many rounds of drinks we reminisced about that very first hotel, at Paddington, where we'd sealed the deal over tea and biscuits. Fifteen years ago . . . And I could still hear Bobby's voice and see his expansive arms: 'Overture to *Don Giovanni* . . . ' Bobby and John didn't look much older, though perhaps a little chastened by experience. They'd lost a lot (as we would discover), but had gained a pet cat, and loved it so much they had flown it with them to Paris. Still the extravagant gestures.

They took us for lunch to Les Amis de Louis, which they called their favourite restaurant in the whole world. We were joined there by their friend and lawyer, Sam Myers, an American in Paris. In late middle age, burly, lawyerly-suited, he looked a tough nut; someone who would have silenced a roomful of Mafia clients in New York if he had not been, as he clearly was, highly respectable. Back at the hotel, he took charge of proceedings, asking Roberdeau to address us. The ever-boyish-looking Roberdeau stood up to give his prepared speech, and seemed slightly abashed, like a schoolboy ordered to stand and read out his inadequate homework. I was fuzzy-headed from fine French food and wine, and took in his speech only vaguely. He appeared to be saying they had made mistakes; in 1994 they had mounted a theatrical event costing $600,000, and one of their main investors pulled out, leaving them unable to cover the cost. They had taken out a loan of $200,000 for three months, from someone called Monty Montgomery, using *The White Hotel* rights as surety. They couldn't make the repayment, so had had to sell the rights to him for one dollar.

We listeners were silent. Roberdeau looked even more embarrassed. I was too confused to take it all in – Andrew had to explain a lot of it later. Otherwise I'd have said, 'Hey, wait a minute, John: you actually *sold* the rights without telling us? For one *dollar*?' Gathering his thoughts, Roberdeau went on to say their friend Sam Myers had come to the rescue. He'd bought the rights back from Montgomery, but promising the boys they could still produce the movie. They would be his employees. We looked at Myers, who nodded. Then, Roberdeau continued, their erstwhile investor, who'd let them down so badly, had brought a stupid lawsuit against them, claiming he owned the rights to all their movie projects; and an equally stupid judge in New York had, incomprehensibly to all sensible people, brought in a verdict against Briarpatch Film Corporation (Geisler and Roberdeau). They were appealing, and would certainly succeed, because that judge had subsequently been debarred. The rights to *The White Hotel* were, John assured us, absolutely ring-fenced against anyone else trying to claim them. A company called Night Hawk, he told us, had been set up, which now incontrovertibly owned the film rights, and they wished to make an offer for a three year option, to begin as soon as the old Briarpatch agreement ran out in July.

Night Hawk made their offer: $50,000 for the first year's option, and the same sum for two further years, subject to conditions insisted on by Myers – mainly, that they sign a director in the first year. 'The boys' were talking to Pedro Almodovar, the great Spanish director. They showed us videos of two of his films, then John said, 'Let's have some more champagne!' Myers snapped, 'No, we've had enough.' Bobby and John looked crestfallen. We shook hands with Myers, and he left. Andrew and I agreed it was good he was in charge; he was solid and reliable, and would obviously keep a grip on things. His watchful presence, as an experienced lawyer, was an additional reassurance that the agreement was *bona fide*.

Our party, *sans* Myers, had a fine, sparkling dinner at a bistro. Bobby and John talked, with their habitual enthusiasm, about Almodovar. 'You'll love Pedro, Don,' Bobby said. 'We're flying on to Madrid to see him; he's very interested. His movies so far have been quite domestic. He's looking for a challenge.' They would send me videos of more of his wonderful movies. I had a cabinet stuffed with videos by Bertolucci, Lynch, Kusturica and others.

Andrew and Margaret and I met for breakfast next morning to discuss the proposed deal. I think they were as bemused as I by what John had told us. For about seven years we had had a contract with Briarpatch, when they hadn't owned the rights any more. I persuaded Andrew to ask for $75,000 on signature. It was a substantial sum; but I was aware that if they had made the movie ten or fifteen years earlier there would have been huge box office interest, and I'd have sold a lot of books. That interest and those prospects had declined drastically. There should be, I thought, some recompense for that – and for selling the rights for a dollar and not telling us. Andrew went off to talk to Bobby and John; when he returned he said they were begging us to split the up front $75,000 into two payments: $50,000 in July, and the remaining $25,000 after six months. Andrew said that clearly Sam Myers was now holding the purse-strings. I agreed to spread the first-year payment.

The Hewsons hosted a lunch, then they returned to London by Eurostar, and I flew home in the little plane, touching down in Jersey en route.

A week or so before the new contract was due to take effect, I received a letter from a New York law firm. The lawyer, one Barry Goldin, was claiming that his client Gerard Rubin owned the rights to *The White Hotel*. Bloody nerve, I thought, and threw the letter in the bin. If there had been a dispute within the Briarpatch camp it was no business of mine; I had played no part in it; I had kept to a legal contract, and now its time was almost up. I had every right to make a new agreement with anyone I chose. And there had been no other offers.

On a beautiful, sunny day in early September 2001, Victoria and I went for lunch at an inn in Restronguet, on the river Fal. It's a lovely creek, where once I used to go for childhood holidays with my parents, staying with their great friend Mona. As we ate our food and drank wine on the jetty, and watched the sunlight shimmering on the water, I remarked how serene it all was. It was impossible to imagine a more serenely lovely day. When we got home, the phone rang almost at once. It was my son Sean, in London. 'Turn on your TV,' he said. I did so. And watched the second plane fly into the Twin Towers.

I rang Ross in Kitchener, Ontario. He sounded sleepy. 'Have you got your TV on?' 'No, why?' 'Just turn it on.' He came back a few moments later. 'Christ! I'd better wake up Carrie.'

A few days later I wrote a card to Bobby and John, expressing my sorrow at the terrible, evil act, and hoped they were okay. They wrote to thank me.

The world was changing, darkening. Karlheinz Stockhausen, interviewed in Hamburg before a concert, said the attack on the Twin Towers was 'the greatest work of art in the history of the entire cosmos'. His stupid, amoral comment angered me deeply, and I wrote a poem, with allusions to Pushkin's *Mozart and Salieri* . . .

Stockhausen's Dream

I have seen many angels, sometimes in human
Form, but not often such an El Greco beauty.
Sit down, and have some wine. Ah no, of course:
Some tea, then? My dear fellow, I'm envious.
I've never before felt envy, neither when
Hearing the *Missa Solemnis*, nor when watching
The Ring at Beyreuth. But now, I envy!
I'm sick with envy, as Salieri was
Of the giggling, childish, farting Mozart. It was
The greatest work of art imaginable
For the whole cosmos. Artists rehearsing like mad
For ten years, preparing for one concert,
And then dying, and 5000 other people
Dispatched to the afterlife in a moment!
The beauty of it, on a September morning,
Itself heartbreakingly beautiful; the planes
So exquisitely timed, white and serene,
Gliding like great condors,
And then, as it were, passing through nature
To eternity, with a shattering of steel and glass!
It took us out of our security
And into a new world, as great art does,
Beyond the limits of what is feasible
Or even conceivable . . . And you did it, Osama!
I couldn't have done it; no composer could.
I used four helicopters in a string quartet
– Maybe you've heard it? – an idea which came
In a dream; but it never occurred to me
To have each pilot nonchalantly tell

His string player they were going to crash
Into the concert hall – and even then
It would have been pathetic . . . Another cup?
It's Earl Grey, rather scented . . .

The dead would give themselves to your masterpiece,
If we could go back. It was their privilege
To watch it in the auditorium,
And tickets, even for my operas, are not cheap.
Who'd have preferred the tedious in-flight movie
To that sudden incandescence? Or, in the Towers,
Who'd choose the dull work and the tuna sandwich
Over that opening up of consciousness?
One moment smiling at some e-mailed joke,
The next, a choice of death by fire or falling.
I loved that *nuance*, the couple hand in hand,
As much as the grandeur of the twin collapse,
The black cloud racing, panic and hysteria.
'Genius and villainy are incompatible,'
Mozart supposedly said to Salieri,
As he drank his poisoned wine. Which is shit,
Of course. Art is above morality.
All the same, I don't like feeling this envy
Which has taken me over, filling me
With hateful thoughts. Is the tea not to your taste?
A slight upset? Come and lie down by me,
Or even in me, which is possible in dreams.

Hell Fire Corner

I still watch my childhood rugby team, the Reds, in working-
class Redruth, ten miles from my home in middle-class,
cathedral-spired Truro. Old loyalties don't die. After the war,
from the age of ten, I would go with my father; after the game,

we'd call in at the sweet-shop run by my aunt Nellie, then go to the Regal to see a film. Actually, two films, since there'd always be a second feature. It was a precious ritual for both of us.

Today, having parked at the rugby ground, trudging around 'Hell Fire Corner' towards the stand, my back aching, head down to avoid slipping on the muddy grass, I hear my name spoken. 'Donald Thomas'. A quiet voice, neither calling to attract my attention nor querying if I'm he, nor even particularly interested; but silkily teasing. I stop and look over my shoulder. A couple of yards up the bank, three elderly men whom I don't know. They could be looking past me rather than at me; I hesitate, wondering if the voice came from somewhere else. Then one of them, with a benign unwrinkled face and a pleasant half-smile, repeated 'Donald Thomas' in the same neutral tone. He waited a few seconds then added, 'Jimmy Glanville.'

'Jimmy Glanville!'

This benign-looking pensioner was Jimmy Glanville!

The last time I saw him was almost sixty years ago. He terrorised me. He was tall, athletic, hard as nails, with a rather cruel face. After school he would harry me up the road towards our homes, which were close to each other, whipping me instead of a hoop, shouting, 'Come **ON**! Come **ON**!' Then, when we played cricket in the nearby croft, he would race in, his features contorted and devilish, and hurl at me from a few paces away the ball we used, which was twice as hard as a cricket ball. Concrete, I believe.

'We used to play cricket together,' I say to his companions.

'You kept blocking and blocking!' says Jimmy, demonstrating with gestures. And the concrete ball, hurled down by him, had wrecked my bat.

'How are you?' I ask.

'Oh, pretty good.'

Jimmy's mother had died when he was a child; I visited him at home just once, and saw his sad-looking, silent father, a railway worker, and felt the coldness and bleakness of the little house which they shared together. I contrasted it, even at eleven, with the warm fire and cosy atmosphere in our bungalow. It was not hard to see why Jimmy had become a bully.

'You were a terrific fast bowler,' I said. 'Terrifying!'

'Was I?'

One of his chums said, 'He's still terrifying,' and they chuckled.

I can see almost nothing of the young Jimmy. He seems shorter than he was in boyhood, as well as incredibly softer. But I see a real resemblance to his father, glimpsed just once.

'Well, nice to see you.' He nods agreement, and I turn and plod on towards the stand.

Before I left Redruth in 1949, to sail with my parents to Australia, I asked Jimmy if he would send me some comics occasionally. He said yes, and kept to his promise beyond the call of duty. Every month, for over a year, a carefully wrapped bundle of *Beano* and *Dandy* comics would arrive at the Melbourne flat, rented by my war bride sister and her husband, where we were 'squatting'. Towards the end I didn't even bother to read the comics, because I'd moved on to the *Sporting World* and *Photoplay*. Sweaty Aussie Rules footballers and Hollywood sweater girls. Looking fat and lethargic, I was charged with sexual energy I didn't know what to do with, living in a world without girls. I was growing intellectually, reading my brother-in-law's books, including a Penguin anthology of new poetry and Roget's *Thesaurus*. What did I have to do with *Beano* any more?

When we returned to England, after two years, we were at different schools and I never set eyes on him. But he has remained always in my psyche, in my mythology. 'Come **ON**! Come **ON**!'

Jimmy Glanville.

Brief Encounter

Another time Denise and I were together very peacefully. It was not long after she had playfully placed my pen in my ashtray. I said, 'We've been together for so many years, it's amazing that we're still in love.'

'Oh no,' she said, 'that's impossible.'

I felt hurt, and withdrew my arm from contact. 'Well,' she added, more gently, 'yes, we are, in a way.'

My arm went round her again, and our cheeks were touching. I could smell the scent of her newly-washed hair. I wanted to tell her again how unique our love was; but then I felt a pang. Could I endure going through her illness and her death again?

But she seemed quite well; perhaps I wouldn't have to endure it.

I took her to the station. It was that familiar *Brief Encounter* parting. I was just gathering myself to tell her how much I loved her when a woman with wild eyes appeared before us on the platform. She went into a ranting speech about how she had had to give me up. She waved her arms and tears sprang to her eyes. It was so over the top – people were staring at her. She marched away, her high heels clattering. Denise and I looked at each other and burst out laughing. 'After all she didn't *have* to come on holiday with us,' Denise said.

'No, she didn't. It was her choice.'

'Excuse me a moment.' And she dashed off through the crowd. I assumed she needed to pee. A train drew in on another platform, waited for people to climb off and on, and left.

She was back beside me. 'I didn't realise how expensive it is to ring France,' she said.

'Who were you ringing?' I asked suspiciously. 'A lover?'

'It's none of your business! You don't own me, you know!

God, you have a wife, and yet you think you have a fucking right to control me! Well, you don't, sunshine!'

'Sorry.' Her train drew in. I took her face in my hands and said, 'I love you so much . . . sometimes it's almost unbearable, the tenderness I feel for you.' I now felt able in these meetings to express fully and romantically the love I'd always felt but often hid – as one does. In any case, she wasn't a woman for romantic gestures. I kissed her, and she melted into my kiss. It was a beautiful, complete embrace. Then she stepped away and got on the train. 'I'll see you next weekend,' I called.

To hell with what my wife would think.

The Medium

'Do you know someone called Sam?' she asked.

I shook my head miserably. None of the names meant anything.

Then she said, 'Did you have a dog?' just as the thought flashed into my mind. 'Yes, we had a dog called Samantha. We often called her Sam.'

She nodded triumphantly. 'She's with Sam.'

Well, that figured. She loved dogs, loved Samantha; and Tamsin, her replacement, who looks very much like Sam.

The medium was in her fifties or sixties, with dishevelled greying hair and a drooping bosom. She was seeing clients in an upstairs room of a pub in St Ives. It was a few weeks after Denise's death. My daughter Caitlin had told me this woman had a good reputation. Caitlin knew the mediums, looking for Alex, her dead little boy.

'She's coming through quite faintly. It takes a while after they die to come through clearly.'

At that moment we heard the whining roar of an automatic drill, outside the window. It sounded as if someone was drilling into the pub wall. Yet, somehow, Denise's voice seemed to be coming through to the medium more clearly. 'She is saying she's in a beautiful garden. And that you had a beautiful garden.'

'Yes.' Denise had created it.

'There are lilies, she says.'

This was interesting. A few months before her death, and before Ross went to Canada, we'd borrowed a video camera and made a home movie to send to Hereford. A daughter of our friends there, Cath and Roger, was getting married. Denise wasn't well enough to go, so we'd come up with this idea of making a video. In one scene I'd pretended to be a rustic gardening expert, showing her around our garden. 'And what are these?' she asked. 'They're nasturtiums,' I said. She'd chuckled. 'They're not nasturtiums, they're lilies!' 'They're not Lily's! They're mine! They're not Lily's! Let Lily get her own flowers.' A desperate attempt at humour. Laughter in the trenches.

Now, was Denise making a smiling reference to that moment?

'She was a very gentle person.'

I snorted: 'She wasn't gentle, she could be very aggressive.'

'Oh, but she was gentle really.'

'That's true.' Gentle to children and animals. Gentle in the vulnerable depths of her. When I confessed I'd fallen in love with someone, I longed for her to show gentleness, since I hated these new feelings, wished to overcome them, and my heart always melted when she showed softness and tenderness; but of course, understandably, she'd shown me only anger.

'Oh, yes! She's laughing, she's saying the boxing gloves were on more than they were off . . . She was very muddled about what she wanted. It wasn't your fault, it was from something in her childhood. But you were muddled too about what you wanted . . . She's saying, if she had her life to live again, she'd have lived it very differently, but she'd still have lived it with you.'

I felt tears sting in my throat. She had used those very words to me, a few months before she died. It was too exact, and the feeling too complex, to be coincidence or telepathy. It had to be Denise. Coming through in spite of the irritating, grinding drill outside.

'Your mother is there. A nice lady. And Denise says she is with her children. Are there children who have passed over?'

'We had a son who was stillborn.'

'Well, she's saying children. She's happy. She's with her children.'

The child she was forced by her mother to have adopted would be about thirty. She never stopped wondering what had happened to him.

A Transatlantic Billet-Doux

In early January 2002, just before I was due to receive the second part of the first-year payment from the newly-created movie company 'Night Hawk', an embarrassed messenger from the Truro City Court handed me a huge parcel. When I opened it I found it was a legal suit against Geisler, Roberdeau, Sam Myers, and me. It was from Barry Goldin, on behalf of his client Gerard Rubin. They were claiming that Rubin, who had taken over Briarpatch, owned the film rights to *The White Hotel*.

I felt very angry that my quiet writing life had been invaded in this way. I skimmed the vast document. My name was hardly mentioned; but Geisler and Roberdeau were accused of manifold crimes of fraud and thievery. I realised this was a part of the legal dispute which Roberdeau had related to us in Paris, six months earlier, and which I had barely understood: but what the fuck did it have to do with me?

The defunct Briarpatch contract was clear. I went rummaging through my madly confused files and at last found it. The relevant clause said: 'REVERSION – If . . . the Purchaser shall have failed to commence principle [*sic*] photography on any motion picture version . . . within that period which terminates on the tenth anniversary of the date of the Purchaser's exercise of the Option . . . then, any and all rights of any nature in and to the Work . . . shall revert automatically to the Author for his sole use and disposition without any further obligation of any kind to the Purchaser.' Hell, it couldn't be clearer!

My first impulse was to write a simple letter to the New York state court at which the legal action was being entered. I would say, 'Your honour, this is an invasion of my rights. I kept faithfully to an agreement with Briarpatch; did nothing wrong; it ended in July 2001, at which point I was free to make another agreement with anyone I chose. Whatever the rights and wrongs of the quarrel between Geisler/Roberdeau and Rubin, I have never played any part in it. I live in Cornwall, England, and have modest means. I could not possibly afford to hire a New York lawyer to represent me in your court. My innocence of any harm done to Mr Rubin is clear-cut; nor does the writ impute any wrongdoing by me. I ask that you dismiss me from the case.'

Then I thought, maybe I should ask my Truro solicitor, Heather Hoskings, who arranged my mortgage, to write the letter. It should be enough, I felt.

As soon as the wintry sun was swimming up in New York, I rang the Geisler-Roberdeau number. John answered. 'It's an entirely frivolous suit,' he said. 'This Goldin is an ass hole; we told you about him.' I said I planned to write to the court myself, or else get my local solicitor to write. – Oh ho ho, no no no! I couldn't do that. 'We've appointed a New York attorney to defend you, Don. He's called Noah Weissman. And he'll work very closely with our lawyer, Paul Verner.'

'*You* appointed a lawyer for me?'

'Yes. Night Hawk will pay for him, don't worry.'

I asked about the $25,000 that was due from Night Hawk in

a few days: the deferred second part of the first-year option payment. No, John said, the agreement was 'tolled' – suspended – until the legal case was resolved. But it shouldn't be long. 'It's entirely frivolous, like I said. We'll put paid to Goldin once and for all!'

It alarmed me to find that I had to write formally to Weissman, hiring him, and promising to pay his fees. Roberdeau assured me it was just a formality – Weissman knew Night Hawk would be responsible. I felt a nagging anxiety nevertheless; and I was agitated when I first spoke to Weissman by phone. I wanted to hear him say the suit against me was as absurd as I felt it to be. 'It's as if I rented someone my house for a month,' I said, 'and at the end of it his raging estranged wife said he'd thrown her out after a week so the lease would have to be extended, without extra payment, so she could live there. It's absurd! Don't you think?'

'It certainly looks that way,' he replied cautiously. He was still mastering the brief, and he was obliged to agree a strategy with Paul Verner, Night Hawk's and Geisler/Roberdeau's attorney.

There turned out to be some disagreement between Weissman and Verner/Geisler/Roberdeau over whether they should try to move the case from the State court to a Federal one. I took part in an absurd three-way phone discussion, between Andrew Hewson in London, me in Cornwall, and Geisler, Roberdeau, Verner and Weissman in New York. I couldn't understand the legal gobbledegook; except that Geisler and Roberdeau wanted Federal because the case would be heard by a Judge Sweet. 'Sweet hates Goldin,' John said; 'he's looking for an opportunity to crush him. We've got to get it before Judge Sweet.' Weissman wasn't sure, and the discussion got nowhere, as far as I could tell.

I've never had the slightest interest in law; have never had the slightest inclination to litigate. Yet here I was plunged into a world where people evidently *enjoyed* the process.

It wasn't long before I was hearing that Geisler and Roberdeau were thoroughly dissatisfied with Weissman. He was slow, costing too much money. And soon I received an e-mail from Verner, instructing me to mail to the court a statement which he had composed. The statement said I was dissatisfied with the competence of Noah Weissman, was dismissing him as my attorney, and appointing in his place – oh, I don't remember his name, I was already thoroughly bemused and fed up. I had no complaint against Weissman, who seemed to me to be honest and intelligent; but I had to go along with Night Hawk's instructions. My letter had to be notarized, then Fedexed. I was having little time or energy for writing.

While I was waiting for an appointment with Truro's only notary public, I received a phone call from Weissman. 'Geisler and Roberdeau are crooks,' he said. 'Goldin would like to meet you and talk to you.'

I was startled; offended on John and Bobby's behalf. I didn't believe they were crooks. They had always dealt with me fairly and generously. I liked them. A money payment might be delayed sometimes, but it always came. I was very angry with Goldin for disturbing my life, interfering with my freedom to earn a living, when I had done absolutely nothing unlawful to harm his client. If Rubin had invested unwisely, that was his look-out. I replied, 'I'm not going to talk to a man who's attacked me for no reason. Tell him he can write to me and I'll consider what he says.'

I don't know if he passed on the message; but I didn't hear from Goldin or Rubin. The case proceeded, indeterminately. Weissman withdrew. I didn't hear much from my new attorney, whoever he was. Occasional e-mails came from Verner and 'the boys', as Andrew, Margaret and I called them. Most of the time I tried to forget that I was being sued for $4.2 million. I found the precision of the sum curious. It was about ten times the amount I had received for the film rights in the whole sixteen Geisler-

Roberdeau years. I still had a mortgage on my home, and a battered old BMW. I joked to friends that I could scarcely afford the four million, let alone the extra two hundred thousand.

The situation defied all reason. If I could have appeared in the New York court personally I would have asked just three questions: Did I ever break my contract with Briarpatch? No. Did that contract legally end in July 2001, with the film rights reverting to me? Yes. Did that leave me free to re-sell the rights? Yes. Yet in the peculiar world of New York law it apparently wasn't at all simple; it was turning into Jarndyce & Jarndyce – *Bleak House*.

'He's *Dead*! He's *Dead*!'

In that spring of 2002, my defence was comprehensively locked into the Night Hawk-Geisler-Roberdeau strategy – whatever it might be. There was no way I could get out of it because they were paying the lawyers. Or possibly not paying them.

One day Andrew, my agent, phoned me, and was not his usual calm, imperturbable self. He sounded quietly agitated. I was puzzled why he was asking me about kidney stones. Yes, I said, they could be very painful, as I well knew. He explained that Margaret had been in intense pain, even rolling round on the floor in agony. They'd thought about kidney stones. They were going to see a consultant.

A few days later, phoning me, he sounded infinitely sad. It was what I had gone through, he said, with Denise. 'Oh God, you mean – !' Cancer. And very advanced; she had been given just a few weeks to live. With treatment, perhaps six months. I called up her image, so gay, so vibrant, and my heart went out to them both, and to their daughter Anna.

It put the lawsuit into perspective. I was too cowardly to go to London to visit Margaret; it would have brought back too many memories of Denise. At Andrew's request, I made a tape of my translations of Pushkin poems, which she loved. She decided to accept chemotherapy, and dealt with her illness with incredible bravery and *style*.

Geisler and Roberdeau were planning to fly over to visit her. Bobby, in a phone call, told me how sad they were for her; and also for their cat, which had just died.

One morning soon after, I was sitting at my desk writing, and listening to the opera *Eugene Onegin*. My phone rang. Slightly irritated to be interrupted, I turned down the music and picked up the phone. The voice I heard was unearthly; I didn't at first recognise it as Bobby's; it was a banshee wail. 'Don, this is Bobby. John is DEAD! he's DEAD!'

Through his sobs he told me how it had happened. They were living in a hotel. John had been parcelling up presentations of *The White Hotel* to send off, yet again, to directors. He left to go somewhere, and had a heart attack in the lobby. He was dead when he reached the hospital. For some reason no one knew who he was. The first Bobby knew of it was after a friend tried to reach John on his cell-phone, and a police officer answered the call.

John was forty eight. Bobby said he was sure the court case had killed him. He had been very fit.

After Bobby rang off, saying he was going to try to sleep, I sat for a long time, still hearing 'He's DEAD! He's DEAD!' I was reminded of a story I had read about Pasternak. One day his mistress, Olga Ivinskaya, model for his Lara, received a phone call from him in which he burst out, through tears, 'He's dead! He's dead!' – referring to his character Yuri Zhivago. But he was fictional, John was real.

I thought of all the effort John had expended, and all the dreams he had dreamed, towards the making of a movie of my book, with Bobby. How sad it was. I saw his perpetually youthful face, heard his boyish chuckle. I started to write a poem, a *sestina*, and over the next couple of days I completed it . . .

Phoning the Dead

Elegy for a Movie Producer

(For John Roberdeau and Bobby Geisler)

My mind was in Russia, thinking of Onegin,
Tatiana's passionate letter, Pushkin's fate.
The phone rang; irritated, I answered it.
John, it was Bobby's voice, but far away
From itself in a torture-chamber, entirely novel,
Entirely out of it: *'John is dead!'*

He'd been crying it all night down the phone: *'He's dead!'*
I clicked off the aria from *Eugene Onegin*;
This was no opera nor verse-novel.
From New York or from Hell I heard your fate:
Heart attack – hotel lobby – carted away;
Cops with your cell-phone the first he knew of it.

We met in a hotel, a station dive. It
Was between trains, I gave you thirty minutes dead.
You sold me yourselves, carried me away
– Like some minor diva suddenly offered Onegin
At La Scala – on your passion. It was your fate,
You urged, to make a great film of my novel.

How many directors threw the novel
Back at you! You were both obsessed with it,
Thwarted for these twenty years by fate,
Losing money, home. When your phone was dead
For months, and I as cynical as Onegin,
You'd spring alive suddenly and again sweep me away!

And all, I thought, like ashes blown away.
Yours will still say, 'We're gonna film that fucking novel!'
That was yesterday. Today I picked up *Onegin*,
Thinking life must go on; opened it

To find an image other than you dead;
And my eyes fell on the last page, by fate:

'So much, so much, has fate
Snatched from us! Blest who early has walked away
From life's feast, leaving his glass of wine not dead;
Who did not read to the end life's novel,
But all at once could part with it
As I with my Onegin.'

You didn't fulfil your dream, like everyone in *Onegin*,
But you'll go on talking, permanent as fate;
When Bobby speaks, you will break into it.

It wasn't completely accurate, I would discover later; a rival obsession had cost them their home. I sent the poem to Bobby, who was touched by it and tried to get it published. He told us there had been some nasty obituaries of John, which upset him greatly. I felt angry too on John's behalf. I felt, if one couldn't speak well of a person just dead, one should say nothing. Unless he were Hitler or a serial killer. Obviously they had made mistakes, and they certainly should have informed me they had sold the movie rights to my novel for a dollar – Christ, it was worth more than that – but I still believed all their actions were in the pursuit of an idealistic dream. I loved his enthusiasm, as I loved Bobby's.

At the next court hearing following his death and funeral, their attorney, Verner, asked for a postponement of two weeks. Goldin, on behalf of his client Rubin, objected, referring to 'the purported death of John Roberdeau'. That phrase, when I read it in a transcript – the only time I was sent one – chilled me to the bone. I could not understand how anyone, whatever his client's grievances, could be so unfeeling. Indeed, it seemed slightly mad. Did he think Roberdeau had been spirited away to Bolivia, like Dr Mengele, or some deserted island, to escape his legal nemesis? Did he think Geisler's overwhelming grief was a charade? It did not endear Goldin to me. It seemed to confirm the Geisler-Roberdeau depiction of him.

Andrew – bearing his own deep pain – and I doubted if Bobby would survive the loss of his partner, as they had been as close as conjoined twins. Bobby doubted it too. His body, substantial yet frail, erupted illnesses. I saw him, in my imagination, rolling along a New York street, unshaven, blown hither and thither like a balloon.

But one day, he told us, he looked at all the packages which John had prepared for sending to directors, and decided John would want him to carry on. He posted the packages. And began courting directors again – Bertolucci, Cronenberg. Even Woody Allen, who responded that he admired the novel but worked only from his own material. A Woody Allen version would have been quite something. He'd make an intriguing Freud.

Probably with Mia Farrow as 'Frau Anna'. One would have to slip in some of the jokes Freud quoted and analysed. Mia, lying on the couch, tells him about her young lodger. He stole into the kitchen while she was making soup for herself and her husband, took her by surprise, kissed her then thrust a hand up her skirt. 'But I forgave him,' she says; 'he's a little crazy.'

Woody, peering at her owlishly through his glasses: 'If he's so crazy, why didn't he kiss the hot stove?'

THREE

On Goldin Pond

Book of the Dead

I was with my parents in Tibet, on a two week holiday. I was planning to drive up Everest as far as we could get by the rough narrow road snaking round the mountain; but thought better of it. I don't like heights; at some point I'd have to turn around, and the road would be so narrow and precipitous I wouldn't be able to. I settled for pointing out the beauty of the Himalayas, tier after tier of white, but my mother wasn't very impressed.

I'd had enough, after a week, of harsh terrain, yak milk and ice. I wanted to go home. What drew me above all was that I'd missed my last date with Denise, having confused when I'd be away. I tried to phone her, but it was difficult getting through from Tibet. I talked to an official, saying I assumed I'd have to return by way of the Trans Siberian Railway, but he said, no, I could fly. It would be expensive, and I would lose the money spent on hotel bookings, but it would be worth it. If I didn't get back, Denise might sleep with someone else, or even finish with me.

I flew home. My face pressed to the window, I could see the peak of Everest below. Denise had envied me my trip. She often talked of visiting Tibet late in life, and she was fascinated by the Tibetan Book of the Dead.

I found her sitting on a beach. She was pleased to see me, and we were warm and loving with each other. Then she took me aback by saying, 'Oh, there's one thing that's happened while we've been apart – I have another child!'

I had to swallow hard. I said, 'Is it —'s?'

She shook her head, then nodded towards a nearby house. 'That stupid sod's.'

Her news had a little dashed my spirits. I said I was worried at having someone else's child to look after, and take on holidays. She said, with a smile, 'Oh, we can leave him behind at home some of the time.'

She was so cheerful and positive about it, I felt reassured. I enjoyed lying with her in the sun, kissing.

A Parfit Gentil Knight

Bobby Geisler spent a day with Victoria and myself in Cornwall, a few months after John Roberdeau's death. He wasn't really with us; he was somewhere beyond this earth; like a dead and swollen-up astronaut who had become detached from the mother spacecraft. We felt deeply for him. I knew exactly how he was feeling: that there had been an amputation of himself from himself. He looked, and felt, physically ill too. We did our best to entertain him, by showing him a bit of Cornwall. He did manage to drink his first glass of wine in months, without feeling nauseous, and said the visit had done him good.

We urged him to stay for longer than a day; but he had plans to go on to Paris, in connection with *The White Hotel*. It was courageous to be hauling himself back into the world of movie making – even if it was movie not-making – on his own, and evidently in financial debt. While I was aggrieved at the lack of communication and consultation in the legal struggle, my loyalties were still firmly with Geisler, a suffering human being, rather than with the Rubin/Goldin camp, whose legal action was depriving me of my livelihood, and whose only response to Geisler's loss had been to oppose a brief deferment and refer to John Roberdeau's 'purported death'.

No doubt Geisler saw Sam Myers – whom Goldin was effectively describing as the *purported* head of Night Hawk – during his trip to Paris. I had had neither sight nor sound of Myers since the jolly weekend in Paris early in 2001. It was painful to think that two of the six people who had gathered for that occasion were now no more, taken in their prime of life.

Andrew announced a memorial service for Margaret, in the autumn of 2002. The date coincided with a surprise Night Hawk 'strategy' conference, at the Savoy Hotel in the Strand, London. I went with Victoria. Sam Myers was there, and clearly paying for most of it. And Verner, Geisler's lawyer, and of course Geisler himself. Another surprise: I was introduced to still another lawyer who was to represent me. One Rick Knight, a Texan, and every inch a Southern gentleman, with a white goatee beard and moustache and gentle manners.

'The boys' had spoken of him before, as a brilliant attorney who had won them some legal victories in Texas. They were in the courts there too – bankruptcy-related, I learned later. Two hours after Margaret's memorial – I'd read two of her favourite Pushkin poems – I sat with Knight in the Savoy lounge as he very painstakingly wrote down some basic facts of the case. It seemed atrocious to me that I was having to go back to basics, nearly a year after the start of the Rubin/Goldin action against me. Knight, writing slowly in his notebook like a schoolboy still uncertain how to join up the letters, struck me *prima facie* as more painstaking than brilliant; but at least he was giving my case some concentrated attention.

The conference as a whole seemed muted and depressed; like a conference of the *Titanic*'s officers, with canapes and champagne, just as the ship was foundering. Myers and Verner – and even Myers' daughter – were now also engulfed in the maw of the Rubin/Goldin action. And against each of us, absurdly in my case, a $4.2 million claim. I had the feeling that if Goldin and Rubin could have traced Bobby's hairdresser, they'd have slapped an action against him too.

At lunch the next day in the Savoy Grill, where I took off my jacket and was immediately asked by a waiter to put it on again, there was a long table of military brass hats near us; a NATO meeting, I believe. At our table, the mood seemed resigned to a long and floundering campaign in the trenches. For some time I had been urging Geisler to take Goldin on, on my behalf, in a British court, feeling that it would be bound to support my right to earn my living without interference. Now there seemed a slight sympathy for this approach.

In the midst of the lunch, during a jovial exchange, spirits briefly lifting along with the wine glasses, Myers growled 'Let's get serious. For instance, who's paying for *this*?' The table grew quiet.

Geisler hosted a concluding dinner at a nearby restaurant. Near the end Rick Knight, who had been mostly silent, burst into eloquent speech. He intended, he said, to serve *my* interests, the interests of his client, *and no one else's*. He emphasised the last phrase, gazing at Bobby at the other end of the table. Geisler looked thunderous, rose from his seat, and stormed out.

I heard no more about Rick Knight's being my attorney. Instead, I was informed by e-mail that one Jules Epstein had been appointed by Night Hawk to represent me. I heard nothing from him, until I insisted on speaking with him. Verner arranged for a Thomas/Epstein/Verner phone conversation. It lasted about three minutes. Epstein said he wasn't familiar with my case, but would soon 'mug it up'. I asked if he thought it would be all over soon, and he responded with a cackle. I had the impression they were both grinning at each other over the naïveté of my question.

To Russia with Love

Feeling guilty because I had never shared one of my great loves with her, I took Denise to Russia. In the confusion of landing and immigration, we became separated and I couldn't find her. Panicking, I decided the best thing I could do was take a taxi to our hotel and just hope she would find it.

I checked in, went to our room, and lay on the bed, feeling awful. What if she had just vanished? What if she didn't know the name of the hotel? At last I heard footsteps, which stopped outside the room, and a knock on the door. I leapt up with relief: it had to be she. And it was. I embraced her joyfully; she held back just a little, turning her lips away. I could see there were still things in our past she had not quite forgiven.

I looked at her as she started moving her clothes from suitcase to chest of drawers and wardrobe. Half her hair was black, as always, and half was white. She looked frail, even though her movements were energetic. I thought, she's probably only got one more year to live . . . Though, she's survived this long – six years – so maybe . . .

She looked very beautiful, and I said, 'You look very beautiful.'

I thought of adding, 'Look, let's get married! Right here in Russia!' It seemed the obvious and lovely thing to do. But then I realised I had married again, and it would be such a hassle to get a divorce.

Later we mingled with the crowds in Red Square. She grasped my hand and said, with a smile, 'This is where we met, thirty years ago!'

I was puzzled when she said it; but later, I realised what she meant. Thirty years ago I had discovered the poetry of Anna Akhmatova. Both women had short black hair and classic features, and they shared the same birthday, June 23.

Probably the Shortest Birthday Present in the World

Two days before my sixty eighth birthday, in January 2003, I received a fax from Geisler that astounded and thrilled me. It read, more or less, 'Don, David Cronenberg has just signed, by fax, to direct the movie of *The White Hotel*. Isn't that wonderful? I talked with David in Toronto recently, and he said to me, Bobby, I know you've been let down in the past over this movie, but I shan't let you down, I promise you. He knows about this frivolous suit and it doesn't bother him. He'd like to write the screenplay himself, and wants to make the movie quickly – this year even. I think he'll do an amazing job. Yours, Bobby.'

I'd met Cronenberg at a dinner party in Toronto a few years before. At the end of the evening he'd brought up *The White Hotel*, saying he felt it was too literary a novel to film. Evidently he had changed his mind. His films were a little dark and bizarre for my taste, but I wasn't going to quibble. Whatever he did with the book, he could hardly out-Potter Potter in infidelity.

I went downstairs, told Victoria the amazing news, and we cracked open a bottle of Tesco Merlot. Over it, we discussed Cronenberg's films; we had seen *Crash* together in a Calgary theatre in '96. Its blackness had fitted in with my mood, as Denise had just lately been diagnosed with terminal cancer. Every night in Calgary I'd dreamt of her ill, dying; and by day I'd had panic attacks – not helped by Calgary's altitude, thinner air and towering skyscrapers, under which I'd felt buried and breathless.

A couple of hours later I was working in my study, my mind still excited. The phone rang. I picked it up and it was Bobby. 'Don,' he said, 'three hours ago David Cronenberg faxed the signed contract to direct *The White Hotel* – '

'Yes, isn't it terrific?'

' – and ten minutes ago he withdrew it.'

'Fuck. *Why?*'

'Oh, Goldin sent him one of his parcels.' His voice sounded infinitely weary and depressed.

'How did Goldin get to hear of it, so quickly?'

'I've no idea.'

We rang off. I could understand Cronenberg's sudden change

of heart. Goldin's massive tomes of relentless legal argument could make the bravest heart quail.

That experience increased my anger against Goldin and his client. If they could have come up with some kind of agreement, a Cronenberg film might have been a chance to recoup some of Rubin's lost money. Instead, they appeared to be trying to prevent a work of art being made. It increased my sympathy for Geisler, who was battling with grief but still trying to *make* an artistic work.

Cruising

We were on a cruise. At some port or other I was told we would have to change ships, and do it in a hurry. Denise and our son Ross weren't in the cabin with me, and I didn't know where they were. A friend of ours, who had some influence with the captain, was arranging to have our luggage taken out and transferred; but just as porters were doing this a whole crowd of people surged into our cabin, and there was chaos. My own two suitcases had gone, I didn't know where. I just hoped they were being loaded onto the right truck onshore; and I was worried that Denise and Ross's luggage would get left behind altogether.

I went looking for them, pushing through the crowds jostling in the ship's corridors and on stairways. At last, to my huge relief, I found Denise, somewhere down in the bowels of the ship. After her absence, she was so solidly, substantially 'there' that I thought, God! I love you so much! If you just knew that, you surely wouldn't worry about my being married, or my flings . . .

We went back to our cabin, which was now empty of luggage and people. All was peaceful; it seemed there was not so much rush after all to disembark. Ross was somewhere away, probably playing the fruit-machines with money Denise had given him.

She and I lay together on a narrow bunk. It had been a long time since I had touched her so intimately. She became wet where I stroked her. She got up to go for a pee; I closed my eyes, waiting for her; but when I opened my eyes I saw that a tiny old woman was standing by the bunk. She mumbled something. She reminded me of the hunchbacked dwarf in the film *Don't Look Now*. Which film reminded me in turn of . . . Donald Sutherland rearing up out of a pool, a child in his arms. Which in turn reminded me of . . . Ross, aged fifteen, rearing up out of our scummy pool, with something in his arms . . .

Creeping away with tiny footsteps, the tiny old woman sat on another bunk under the port-hole. Denise came back, and I asked her who the old woman was. She said, 'Oh, I met her on deck; she seemed lonely, so I invited her to join us sometime.'

I was disappointed; we wouldn't be able to make love; but I appreciated that Denise was being thoughtful.

We drew near to the end of our voyage. I said to her, 'But you've really enjoyed the trip, haven't you? And Ross?' She said yes, but in a slightly grumbly tone, which disappointed me again. As we were disembarking, I noticed a friend of my wife's. She saw me too, and drew me aside. 'Come and see me,' she said, her eyes seductive. 'My phone number is Zennor 285. Can you remember it? Tomorrow would be good. Do come.' She sidled back into her part of the queue to get off.

I felt flattered by her approach. And she looked more attractive than I'd ever thought her before – tanned from the trip, and invigorated. I thought, Denise will be tired; she probably won't mind my driving to Zennor, on some sort of writerly business. It would be good to go to Zennor, even without the sexual temptation. It has the magic of the ancient Celtic fields and carns, and the mermaid in the church holding a mirror, who lured men down away with her singing and drowned them in her ocean of enchantment. Denise and I, early in our relationship, had spent beautiful secret holidays in that part of Cornwall. Nights of deep drowning in the lonely holiday cottage.

'I forgot to mention, I need to go to Zennor tomorrow.'

'Oh, do you? What for?'

'I promised to collaborate with an artist down there.'

She seems satisfied. I'll go, and entwine with the mermaid again, whom I call Kerenza, the ancient Cornish for love.

Break-ups

It was a long time before I began to get any sort of grasp on the legal situation in New York. Goldin's documents were too vast and impenetrably legalistic; my own *purported* attorney, Epstein, was still 'mugging it up', or at least not communicating. But at length, through the pea-souper, a few vague shapes emerged . . .

The 1999 New York court judgement had said that Geisler/ Roberdeau owed Rubin $1.8 million, having defrauded him, and awarded him the Briarpatch company and all their movie projects, including *The White Hotel*. Rubin now owned Briarpatch. However, in 1999 Geisler/Roberdeau no longer owned the movie rights to my novel, having sold them several years earlier, in 1994, for one dollar to Monty Montgomery. Subsequently their friend and lawyer, Sam Myers, had bought the rights from Montgomery. On those grounds, Geisler/Roberdeau could argue that the 1999 judgement could not touch *The White Hotel* project. It was Sam Myers, as owner of Night Hawk, who made the option agreement of 2001 with me. Night Hawk would merely employ Geisler/Roberdeau to produce the movie.

Nonsense, argued Goldin/Rubin, Myers was only a 'straw' for Geisler/Roberdeau. Night Hawk itself was an unreal company, suspiciously based in Gibraltar, existing only to cheat Rubin of his rights to my novel. Goldin was attempting to persuade the court to enforce 'discovery' of all the documents, e-mails, faxes, etc., involving Night Hawk, Geisler, Myers, Verner, Night Hawk's lawyer in Gibraltar, Andrew Hewson, me – believing they would prove his point.

I was unfamiliar with the legal sense of 'discovery'. For me, Columbus discovered America; but in legal-speak America 'discovered to' Columbus. I hated it. I didn't *discover* until much later that, in May 2003, Night Hawk and D. M. Thomas tried to have the case against them dismissed in the District (Federal) Court of their favourite Judge, Sweet, but failed because Night Hawk was unwilling to 'discover'. Then Night Hawk tried again in December, this time dismissing themselves from the case, leaving just 'D. M. Thomas and D. M. Thomas Ltd' (I had once briefly and foolishly been a limited company); but the good judge insisted that Night Hawk 'was an indispensable party'. It was many weeks before I somehow or other got word of this. Geisler, in a phone call to Andrew Hewson, blamed Verner, Night Hawk's attorney, for idleness in preparing the papers; Verner let it be known he'd found it hard to get hold of Geisler.

There was increasing dissent in the Night Hawk camp, a sign of faltering morale. And Geisler became more and more difficult to find. Andrew tried several times to make contact with him in the early months of 2004, but failed. His mailbox was always full. Myers too was elusive. Another crucial date was approaching: July 11 2004. That would mark the end of the three-year Night Hawk option. We wanted to know if they intended to ask for an extension. If so, they would have to find a lot of money. I'd received nothing for almost two years, because of the 'tolling' of our agreement.

We had no replies to our urgent messages.

Then, one spring day, another Potter entered the scene. Susan Stewart Potter – no relation to Dennis – who rang me and introduced herself as an independent producer and writer, living in California. In a rich, musical voice, she asked if the movie rights to *The White Hotel* were available. She was looking for a project, and had happened to find my book in a second hand bookstore. She had never forgotten it from her first reading, fifteen years earlier, and believed it could be a real, emotional film, with a powerful heroine, unlike the vapid action stuff Hollywood was churning out.

I explained the situation, including my sense of helplessness at being trapped. She said she'd read about the court action in the LA Reporter. Maybe if she and I made an approach to Goldin something could be worked out; like a three-way agreement. 'Then I'll make the movie!' Geisler would never make it, she said; on the whole the people in the industry were honest, because their careers depended on their reputation. Geisler didn't have a good reputation.

I could be interested, I said, but I could do nothing until the Night Hawk option ended. We agreed to talk again. And after two or three more calls and e-mails I began to like her confidence, and the ring of sincerity and passion for film-making in her speech. But she was clearly fairly new on the scene; I couldn't find her company, JOA Productions, on the internet. She said she was just setting a website up.

Having talked to Andrew, we decided to consult a London lawyer who specialises in copyright, Bernard Nyman. I had used him once before, long ago, very satisfactorily. Nyman looked at my Night Hawk agreement and advised that I had every right to consider it at an end when the option period was up. He didn't think it should ever have been 'tolled' by Night Hawk.

We waited to see if Geisler or Myers would contact us about an extension. Nothing came. Bobby seemed to have gone to ground.

I managed at long last to get hold of some court records and transcripts. District Judge Sweet's pronouncements showed a superior mind and literary style. He wrote of the 'maelstrom of litigation' . . . 'Characteristically, as in any well developed maelstrom, there are actions and counteractions.' He referred, surely with irony, to Goldin/Rubin 'alleging modestly' thirteen causes of action. In a short section called *The Controversy*, he writes:

> This action is the latest of at least eleven (and possibly more) actions and proceedings which evolve from an investment made by Rubin in Briarpatch, an entity created by Robert Geisler and John Roberdeau who, according to Rubin, swindled him, Briarpatch, and its affiliated enterprises. The instant litigation against Geisler and Roberdeau in the State court was resolved by a judgement in Rubin's favour, and the remainder of the litigation is the effluvia of that judgement, exacerbated by the ill-will of the parties and excessive and occasionally misguided zeal of their lawyers.
>
> Fortunately for the purposes of the pending motions it is not necessary to descend into the briarpatch of the parties' underlying contentions and to parse the rights of what could be valuable properties if the litigation could ever be properly resolved.

My God, I thought, this man should be a novelist. Here was a readable, indeed elegant, legal judgement! I had only ever been able to skim Goldin's documents – apart from the infrequent times when I was mentioned specifically – because they were so long, so impenetrable, so zealous. I was glad Sweet had noted the 'excessive and occasionally misguided zeal', on both sides. If only Goldin had shown an occasional lightness and wit, such as Sweet's use of briarpatch as a metaphor, or his 'alleging modestly' thirteen crimes – probably more than Goering faced at Nuremburg.

But then, I reminded myself, one does not expect lightness, wit, irony, from either an anaconda or a lawyer, and Goldin's *forte* was total, overwhelming constriction. He was a Field Marshal Haig, not a Nelson (I was reading lots of war books at the time). Goldin would no doubt counter, fairly enough, that he was just being a highly efficient and legally scrupulous lawyer serving his client.

Sweet quoted the indisputable clause by which the Briarpatch rights had reverted to me in 2001, and I remembered 'the boys' saying the judge had once remarked to Goldin, informally, that he would always declare that 'the rights had reverted to D. M. Thomas'. As I interpreted his judgement, he could not find for me in this action simply because Night Hawk had refused to 'discover' documents; and since we were tied together in an agreement they were an indispensable party.

I was completely trapped. The courts wouldn't find for me unless Geisler, Myers *et al* gave discovery. And it looked as if they would never willingly do that. Verner, Geisler's lawyer, was himself being sued by Goldin/Rubin, creating a conflict of interest which added to the complication.

I started to reread *Bleak House*; and – even though I had once rather unwillingly taught the novel in a grammar school – I now understood it for the first time. In my bones. 'Jarndyce and Jarndyce droned on. This scarecrow of a suit has, in course of time, become so complicated that no man alive knows what it means. The parties to it understand it least; but it has been observed that no two Chancery lawyers can talk about it for five minutes without coming to a total disagreement as to all the premises . . . ' For all I knew, Briarpatch v. Briarpatch might actually be a continuation of the Jarndyce & Jardyce action.

I read transcripts of subsequent court proceedings, now back in the State court under Judge Karla Moskowitz, in which everyone (except doubtless Goldin) seemed to have sunk into a Dickensian stupor. The judge mislaid her papers; had to ask who was representing me. I could imagine her and the lawsuit transferred to a higher court . . .

Supreme Court of Heaven

Briarpatch Limited, L. P. and Gerard F. Rubin Esq. – Plaintiffs
Index No. 8502847613
– against –
Robert M. Geisler et al., D. M. Thomas,
D. M. Thomas Ltd. – Defendants.
–before–
The Honourable Holy Sophia, Justice

THE COURT	All right, let's make a start. In the courtroom is . . . ?
MR URIEL	Archangel Uriel. I am counsel for the plaintiffs Briarpatch Limited, LP, and its limited and sole winding-up partner, Gerard F. Rubin.
THE COURT	And who is speaking for Mr Thomas?
MR SHEMUEL	I am, your Honour.
THE COURT	I have here a fax from him . . . Did you receive a fax?
MR SHEMUEL	I'm not sure, your Honour, I've been working from home.
THE COURT	Well, that's your problem. Well, the fax says . . . Just a minute, I don't seem to have the papers . . .
MR URIEL	He was never apprised by Mr Shemuel of any stay of application.
THE COURT	And was Lady Dedlock apprised?
MR URIEL	I believe so, your Honor.
MR GABRIEL	The issue today, I thought, was the TRO portion of the request of the Order to Show Cause. I am also concerned that referee Ishmael is pressing Mr Geisler in the primary action to proceed forward with this accounting situation. I am also concerned that nearly immediately after we left the court at the last appearance, where your

Honor made it clear that you were going to try not to take any action in these cases until my counsel's motion to dismiss the action against me were determined, we received default motions from Mr Uriel as against Mr Geisler and Night Hawk.

THE COURT Is Night Hawk present? I'm sorry, I don't seem to have my papers, I must have left them upstairs.

MR SHEMUEL Night Hawk is not an entity, your Honor.

MR URIEL Night Hawk has no existence.

MR GABRIEL Night Hawk stands on its own with respect that motion for default. However, as to Mr Geisler in this action, what we call the D. M. Thomas action and the White Hotel action, again, I am in the same position both with respect to the accounting in the first action and the default now sought in this action. I just need some clarity whether I have an actual conflict of interest, which will be determined when your Honor determines whether I remain a party in this litigation or I am dismissed.

THE COURT I wish I had my papers. There are two orders to show cause, am I right?

MR URIEL Correct, your Honour. 603820 of '99 and 603364 of '01.

THE COURT Since notice was not given to everyone in the lawsuit in the '01 action – and I can't remember the parties, actually, in the '99 action.

MR GABRIEL That would be Geisler, the reincarnated John Roberdeau –

MR URIEL Purportedly reincarnated. We don't know where he is.

MR GABRIEL – Briarpatch Film Corporation, Samuel Myers, and his daughter, Claudia Myers.

THE COURT	Briarpatch is bringing this action, am I correct? So why did you say Briarpatch is the defendant? – Oh yes, I see. Since not everyone got notice in the '01 action, which is D. M. Thomas and D. M. Thomas Limited –
MR GABRIEL	Well, I assume he is pro se at this point and I'm sure we can take care of that notice issue.
THE COURT	Fine. So every opposition should be in everybody's hands by Armageddon, and I'll hear the motion next day.
MR GABRIEL	And what time will that be, your Honor?
THE COURT	Third millennium.
MR GABRIEL	Thank you, your Honour.
THE COURT	I am concerned to move this action forward. It was already old when Mr Jarndyce was alive. It's been in process now for – how long is it?
MR SHEMUEL	Six trillion years, your Honour.
THE COURT	Six trillion years. Well, that's a long time. So I want any opposition to the motion to show cause to be in my hands by the Day of Judgement at latest.
MR GABRIEL	Understood. If we can find Mr Geisler. It is very difficult to find Mr Geisler.

I received a moving letter from another author who felt ground to dust between the remorseless antagonists. He had read an article I wrote for the *Guardian*, London, called 'Celluloid Dreams'. This man had walked, as it were, in my moccasins. He told me he was wined and dined by Geisler and Roberdeau, then paid for a screenplay draft with a dud cheque. On the grounds that the cheque had been good when they mailed it – though not when the author cashed it – Geisler and Roberdeau still claimed the movie rights; and Geisler screamed down the phone that he'd ruin him if he didn't concede.

His agents managed to extricate him from this, and got him a new deal. It would mean several hundred thousand dollars, more money than he'd ever earned. Then along came an Exocet in the form of 'a vast file of legal documents', claiming Rubin owned the rights. 'The new deal was theirs. Theirs with no compensation to me and with no time limit for any other deals they may make. Theirs without any contractual restrictions or obligations – and theirs forever.' Immediately the film company which had bought the rights backed off, putting the project in limbo.

He concluded his letter: 'I found your account heart-wrenching – especially the fact that you lost your wife along the way. Everything you say about seeing your "calm" destroyed is exactly my feeling. I have never had to deal with legal action. Neither my wife nor I have the health or stamina to take on a burden like this. I am frankly way out of my depth and not even sure I can afford to hire the legal brains I need to avoid financial loss. I simply want the whole mess to go away.'

Wilfully and Contumaciously

Suddenly, in June 2004, I read a court transcript – already several weeks old – which stunned me:

> **Notice**: THE PURPOSE OF THE HEARING IS TO PUNISH DEFENDANTS D. M. THOMAS AND D. M. THOMAS LTD FOR CONTEMPT OF COURT FOR HAVING WILFULLY AND CONTUMACIOUSLY IMPAIRED, IMPEDED AND FAILED TO OBEY THIS COURT'S LAWFUL MARCH 17 2004 DISCOVERY ORDER AND FOR HAVING DEFEATED, IMPEDED, IMPAIRED AND OTHERWISE PREJUDICED PLAINTIFF'S RIGHTS AND THAT PUNISHMENT THEREFORE MAY CONSIST OF FINE OR IMPRISONMENT, OR BOTH, ACCORDING TO LAW.
>
> **Warning**: YOUR FAILURE TO APPEAR IN COURT MAY RESULT IN YOUR IMMEDIATE ARREST AND IMPRISON-MENT FOR CONTEMPT OF COURT.

I had a momentary vision of Judge Karla Moskowitz stepping down from the bench, removing her gown to reveal a corset and black stockings, asking the clerk for a whip, and proceeding to **punish** me. But this was no fantasy scene; I was in contempt of court, having been under a legal command to make discovery since March, and *my attorney had not told me!* He had not called me to say, 'Mr Thomas, you're required to make discovery.' I would have had no problem, I had nothing to hide. The real contempt was on the part of the 'Night Hawk' legal team, towards me.

That made up my mind. The next court hearing had been set for late July 2004. Taking instructions from Nyman, my London lawyer, on July 12 I wrote to Night Hawk saying their option had lapsed; to 'my' New York attorney dismissing him; to Judge Moskowitz confirming this; and to Barry Goldin, saying I was willing to negotiate.

It wasn't without a pang that I parted company with Bobby Geisler and the continuing presence of John Roberdeau. It was like the break-up of a long marriage. We had been in a sense friends for eighteen years. I had enjoyed their company, their enthusiasm and their generous hospitality. Unfortunately, someone else usually had been paying for it.

Break-ups were in the air. My marriage to Victoria, after four years, was gently but surely coming apart. She was and is beautiful, idealistic and talented. We had loved each other. I felt very sad it hadn't worked out. There are ten thousand interwoven strands in any marriage; it's impossible for any outside to understand what is going on – and even more impossible for those inside. One strand in ours had been the after-effect of Denise, my grief and remorse for things done and things left undone. As Rosmer and Rebecca find out in Ibsen's *Rosmersholm*, the ghosts of former wives are hard to ignore.

A New Life

Victoria and I were at a party, where we got talking to a rather pompous man. He revealed that he was dating a woman called Denise. I questioned him, and it became clear she was *my* Denise. It was a shock. We had not met for so long I'd thought she must have died. She had come through her illness after all! My heart raced. I wanted desperately to have her with me again. I explained to the man that I knew her, very well.

Aware that I was being tactless in my wife's presence, I said to him, 'If I write a letter would you give it to her? There are things I want to say to her.'

'I'll tell her you've asked if she would receive your letter.' Pompous prick!

'Thank you.' I realised he would probably 'forget' it; and if he mentioned me to her it would lack the persuasiveness of my own words. But I had to be content with this. 'She's in a new life now, of course,' I added.

'Yes, Leicester.'

A pretty grim industrial city in the Midlands. Would she be happy there? I imagined she was teaching again.

I said lightly, boldly, 'I suppose she's still wearing stockings and suspenders?'

He smiled. 'Oh yes! I'm trying to persuade her to be more modern, but she's still wearing them, as of yesterday.'

How fucking ironic, I thought – she's sleeping with a man who doesn't like stockings and suspenders!

Rooming with Lawyers

Following my letters of July 12 2004, dismissing Night Hawk and Jules Epstein, Andrew Hewson and I received – by fax, e-mail and phone – distress calls from Geisler. Bernie Nyman advised us to refer everything to him. Geisler became increasingly threatening. His attorney, Verner, wrote that I was being emotional, and sneered that I wanted my attorney to 'hold my hand'. No, I just wanted to be informed and consulted. That's what lawyers do with their clients. I always thought they especially did so if they were under threat of imprisonment for contempt of court.

Jules Epstein, 'my' attorney, responded to my dismissal of him with a surprisingly warm little note. He wished me well. I felt he was probably heartily relieved to be relieved.

Goldin proved willing to talk. We might explore a three-way agreement with Susan Potter. In the middle of July I was in the habit of spending a week in Toronto, running a creative writing workshop at Humber College. Humber, a large community college with a flourishing creative writing department, treats the visiting authors so generously, with unlimited hotel expenditure for them and their consorts, business class flights and limo travel, that no author ever withdraws. Consequently we are all extremely old. They will soon be meeting our flights with bath chairs. They probably have oxygen machines and a funeral parlour at the ready, in case. Indeed, I know they have a funeral parlour ready, since the first time I went, and tried to find my classroom in the maze of corridors, I ended up abruptly at the end of a basement cul de sac, faced with a sign saying Funerary Arts.

This year, my visit would provide a great opportunity for Goldin, Susan Potter and myself to meet for an evening of 'exploration'. It would be a suitable time and venue, since Goldin/Rubin had barred my creative path as abruptly as I'd been barred by Funerary Arts. Skilfully Goldin had embalmed the Geisler-Roberdeau movie project.

Goldin flew in from New York and Potter from LA, booking rooms at the Park Hyatt Hotel where the authors were being luxuriously housed.

I met Susan first. She proved in person to be a little,

attractive, pink-cheeked lady, with spiky blonde hair, a wide piskyish smile and a floaty dress. In her early sixties, but looking younger, in the Californian way. There was something lightsome about her, floaty like her dress; I felt if she spread her arms she would take flight. I thought she could audition for the part of Moth or Mustardseed in *A Midsummer Night's Dream*. We greeted each other affectionately, having talked a lot by phone and e-mail. When she laughed at some joke, it was like a foghorn, or Ethel Merman.

Barry Goldin, in person, was tall, trim, rather stiff and conservative in appearance, softly spoken and courteous. Not at all like an anaconda, though his eyes were glittering and intensely focused. He said it was an honour to meet me. We ate dinner *al fresco* at a restaurant, so I could smoke; and carried on serious discussions back in my room, over mini-bar drinks. Goldin was amenable to a three-way agreement, but adamant that he would hold all the aces. If he and I could come to an agreement, then he would see if he could make one with Susan – and if so, she and I could make what agreement we pleased.

Despite his polite and softly spoken manner, he focused lasar-like on the proposed agreement with me. This was no surprise, of course. I thought he probably spent all his waking hours in the pursuit of Geisler for the sake of his client, who he felt had been grievously wronged.

I asked him why it had been necessary to refer in court to 'the purported death' of Roberdeau. He looked slightly uncomfortable for an instant; then replied that they were such fraudsters he'd genuinely wondered if Roberdeau had really died. He clearly had a picture in his mind of John still alive on a beach in Hawaii, in a hut in the Andes, or in some cave on the Galapagos Islands. But couldn't he have checked with the hospital or funeral parlour, then expressed his formal condolences? There is a place for the common decencies surely, even in a New York court.

I hoped, with *The White Hotel* gone, Geisler might be able to restart his life. I said to Goldin, 'If we can come to an agreement, would you end the lawsuit against Geisler? You'll have what you want, and Geisler is alone and broke.' Goldin replied to the effect that there would be a law of diminishing returns for further court action. I had to be content with that.

As our evening drew to an end, he said, 'I've brought a large file of documents with me for you to read. I imagine you won't want to take it with you? Shall I Fedex it?'

No, I wouldn't want to take it on the flight. His file would require a separate cargo plane. 'Send it to Bernie Nyman,' I said.

Before I flew back to England I spent a weekend with my son Ross in Kitchener, not far from Toronto. It was good to see him again, with his wife Carrie and his three stepchildren – two teenage girls and one six-year-old, Anna, who looked upon him as her dad and whom he clearly loved like a father. After Ross and Carrie had 'met' on an internet chat-room, during his mother's illness, he'd visited her and they'd fallen in love. She was twelve years older, sober and sensible, and a godsend to him in his grief. Carrie had a managerial job in the post office, and Ross was house-husband. I felt that boredom was eating at him, in the quiet suburb of a sober Germanic town, but he'd have been far too loyal to tell me.

He seemed pleased to see me. Our relationship hadn't been easy in earlier years, but I felt it was beginning to warm. I just hoped he knew how much I loved him.

When I arrived home I rang Susan Potter in California to compare notes on our meeting, then reported to Andrew and Bernie. Bernie received Goldin's Fedex. 'It's enormous!' he chuckled down the phone. He said he would read it and get back to me. A couple of days later he rang again. 'I've been reading all about Geisler and Roberdeau,' he said. 'I'm shocked!' He recounted a list of their alleged financial misdeeds.

His reaction, so unlike his normal cautious, lawyerly (British lawyerly), gentlemanly manner, shocked *me*. I'd not believed Weissman, my first Night Hawk-appointed lawyer, when he'd called them crooks – not only because of long friendship and persuasive explanations, but because Goldin's attacks were so extreme. Since then I had accepted that Geisler and Roberdeau had probably treated Rubin badly – but then, if you make an investment you're taking risks. But now I had to adjust to the possibility that Bobby and John, whom I thought I knew so well and liked, had (in the blunt word used by Judge Sweet, summarising the 1999 judgement) swindled people.

There followed an excruciating four months, trying to negotiate a 'Motion Picture Rights Agreement 2004'. In 1985, a short while after Maureen left me, I had visited a clairvoyant who lived on a council estate. The woman knew nothing of me, and didn't read books. She told me some astonishing things. For instance, that I would have to have an operation in a few months. I did: from feeling perfectly healthy I found myself needing to have urgent operations to remove kidney stones. She said I would be involved in buying or selling three houses. I would be, a year later: selling my Hereford house and a small holiday house, and buying the Cornish house I live in now. And there was much else that was true, or would become so. But she said one thing which seemed comically unlikely, that I would be 'surrounded by lawyers'. I've always avoided seeing a lawyer if I could possibly do so. And I'd largely succeeded. The occasional visit to arrange a mortgage or an agreed divorce – that was all.

But now, in late 2004, it came true. I sat in my Cornish study with two lawyers in almost constant virtual attendance: Bernie Nyman and Barry Goldin. Susan Potter's lawyer also popped in now and again. Almost every hour my old-fashioned fax ground out an endless stream of paper: usually the latest draft from Goldin, or Nyman's suggested amendment to it. Goldin seemed incapable of faxing fewer than thirty pages a time. My study became buried in rolls and scrolls of faxes. Truro ran out of the antiquated fax rolls I still used. Its one notary public saw so much of me, when documents had to be notarised and Fedexed, that we almost became friends, we were on the verge of inviting each other to dinner. I could foresee us going on foreign holidays together, with our spouses. Goldin was clearly a man of integrity, since Nyman was impressed by him; but negotiating with him was an exhausting business, like trying to argue with a *tsunami*. My head was filled, not with thoughts of the next page of a novel, or lines of Frost or Yeats, but legalistic phrases.

Goldin was intent on striking a hard bargain. He thought Rubin was owed it. They genuinely believed – it now emerged – or appeared to, from Goldin's vehement written assault – that I had conducted secret negotiations in a conspiracy with Geisler and Roberdeau. A charge which wasn't true and for which there was no evidence. I'd made the deal in the Paris weekend in the presence of my morally impeccable Scottish agents and a reputable, high-powered lawyer, Myers. I'd never made a secret of my Night Hawk agreement, and could scarcely 'conspire' to sell the rights when they were mine to sell and there was no other offer on the table.

I think Goldin and Rubin could not imagine how a writer, even in Britain, would not have a direct line to all the legal judgements and movie magazines and gossip in America. Writing, after all, was business – what else could it be? They pictured me in daily contact with my attorney, my agent, my broker.

But when I'm writing, I'm in daily contact only with my Muse. Though too often she is busy, and asks me to leave a message and she'll get back to me. The Muse took a sabbatical during those months.

Bernie was a model of patience, and devoted inordinate time to my affairs. It was an expensive negotiation, though I believe he charged me much less than he might have done. He tempered the wind to the shorn lamb.

Goldin was insistent that Rubin should have the movie rights for over six years: the amount of time that had remained on the Briarpatch contract when Geisler and Roberdeau first – according to the New York judgment – defrauded him. I couldn't see the logic of my being made to suffer for wrong-doing *within* the Briarpatch camp, for which I had no responsibility and about which I had known nothing. But Goldin was immovable. And if I didn't accept, his action against me would continue, and I'd have to pay for a New York attorney. In a case which would go on and on, in deadlock. I had no alternative.

Throughout this dismal period I was consoled by Susan Potter's bubbling enthusiasm to make the movie. There was intense interest, she said. She herself had moments of hysteria when she wondered if she could ever make an agreement with Goldin. We always used his name, because his client, Rubin, never appeared. For all we knew, he could have been a chimera, the 'purported Gerard Rubin'. Goldin was insisting that, if Susan's company JOA managed to get finance together for a film, Rubin should be fully recompensed for his investment losses. $3 million would go to him, whatever the movie's budget. Unsure from day to day whether there would be an agreement, Susan nevertheless wrote a new screenplay. That showed real commitment. She also, late on – much too late for me to have second thoughts – reduced by 75 per cent the sum she had agreed to pay me up front, saying her lawyer had told her she couldn't afford so much.

Her lawyer, in fact, was advising her not to sign with Goldin. The terms were too one-sided. Apart from the heavy pay-off, he would only grant JOA a firm one-year option, though he *might* extend it if he felt there was progress. Caught up in her passion, and with the screenplay already written, Potter rejected his advice, and her lawyer resigned. She hired a new lawyer.

Keeping the pressure on, Goldin was also insisting there be a deadline for agreement, 13 December 2004. That last day was frantic; Bernie was in his office until one in the morning. When he tried to reach Susan's lawyer, he was told she had gone to buy some Chinese medicine. He rang me, I rang Susan, her husband answered, said she wasn't in, gave me her cell-phone number, I called her, she was hysterical, she called her attorney, her attorney called Bernie, Bernie called Goldin . . . And at last it was done. I collapsed exhausted, and I imagine Bernie did too. And maybe Susan. Probably only Goldin, who'd got what he wanted, and Susan's lawyer, re-invigorated by Chinese medicine, did not.

Rubin (Briarpatch Ltd.) had the rights for six plus years; they were granting JOA Productions an option for one year. I would get some money from JOA. And Rubin/Goldin/Briarpatch would drop their action against me once I had 'made discovery'. This involved Andrew Hewson having to travel to Gloucestershire and delving into the cobwebbed vault where he stored ancient files.

For Goldin, the essential prize was the Agreement with me. If JOA made the film – possibly against his expectation, given Potter's inexperience and lack of movie prestige – and delivered the pay-off, then great; but if they didn't, he had five more years. For me, it was a business deal, a necessary one in order to climb out from under Bleak Hotel. With Geisler and Roberdeau it had been, at first, a journey, an adventure. 'The Overture to *Don Giovanni* . . . Can't you hear it, Don? . . . ' His arm waving, his eyes visionary, joyous. ' Lisa in the train going to the white hotel . . . '

It might have felt different if I had had any personal contact with Gerard Rubin. I think I met him once, on my first visit to New York for Bobby and John. They introduced me to a chubby, smiling, black-suited man, saying he was an important investor. There were so many people milling around, and I was shaking so many hands, that I didn't catch his name. But surely it was Rubin. Since that time, however, the man who now owned the film rights to my novel has never bothered to address me, except through Goldin's legal-speak. Inevitably I saw him as interested only in the finance, in getting his money back. Art as investment. It might not be true, but he had given me no reason to believe otherwise. No doubt he is an honourable, kind, decent human being, but he has never shown me his human face

Tricksters

I'd asked Bernie to send me the huge Goldin dossier. One-sided though it was, it did provide a picturesque account of Geisler and Roberdeau's way of life, from 1994 on. With Rubin they had taken the line, 'If you're not with us to the end – tough.' And that seemed to become general: 'If you stick with us to the end, you'll get paid; if you pull out, you'll see nothing.'

Geisler told Robert Kolker, of New York Metro, 'We've made some mistakes. Survival isn't easy. Sometimes it involves cannibalism.' The amount of litigation against them or their companies had become enormous, even apart from the Briarpatch briarpatch. It included an uncontested conviction for theft of $20,000 against a travel company: Roberdeau paid by cheque then immediately cancelled it; a woman from Ohio who invested $15,000, to whom punitive damages were awarded; a location scout who claimed he wasn't paid $16,000. Jane Weinstock, who rented them a flat in Gotham, claimed she was left after months with $25,000 of unpaid rent, a $2,000 phone bill, a cable TV bill and a broken mirror. Dennis Potter's estate was claiming $75,000. Geisler was held in contempt of court three times, but always managed to stall procedures by declaring bankruptcy or by other legal means.

Geisler says he and Roberdeau have had to spend over a million dollars in legal fees over the years. Perhaps 'spend' really means 'run up', because numerous lawyers allegedly remained unpaid. One of them, Marc Israel, a partner in a small (two-man) firm in New York, brought a suit in 1997 for $175,000. He had defended them in fifteen or more lawsuits. He testified that by the time he realised 'not paying their debts was simply their way of doing business' he could only go on in the hope that their film, *The Thin Red Line*, would actually happen. Roberdeau, he alleged, kept telling him 'only those who cross the finishing line with us will get paid'.

Then the film *did* get made; and Roberdeau, according to Israel, told him 'he was actively arranging to have any monies that were to be paid . . . deposited into accounts that "nobody can ever get to".' Including, Israel presumed, himself. He said he was desperate; the bills owed were much larger than he had ever earned in a single year. He and his wife had been hoping to buy a home, but now it looked out of reach. Reading this, for the first time in my life I felt sorry for a lawyer.

What, one wonders, did 'waiting to the end', 'to the finishing line', mean to Geisler and Roberdeau? *The Thin Red Line* had been made, and they'd been paid $1.5 million. In their world, it would seem, artists would be paid and treated generously, even lavishly; but caterers, lawyers, landladies, travel agents, needn't be.

And yet . . . I can't believe words like 'scoundrels' and 'crooks' can sum them up. They were also generous, warm-hearted, and passionate about film. They could radiate energy and a vision. Their grief for Margaret Hewson was heartfelt, I know. Geisler still has loyal friends.

He has claimed there were no financial 'mistakes' before 1993. But then, perhaps there didn't need to be, since Rubin was bank rolling them to the tune of millions. When he pulled out, and they lost home, furniture and possessions, and had to move into a hotel – not a white one – I think a kind of insanity may have taken possession of them. They weren't going to let penury stop them in their quest for a filmic holy grail. They had lived in so many dreams of fantastic movie scenes that the characters who bounced cheques and didn't pay lawyers were like fictional projections from their real, honest and likeable selves.

These shadow-selves, as I see it, were like the tricksters of mythology. The trickster deities break the rules of the gods or nature, with tricks or thievery, sometimes maliciously (for example, Loki) but usually with ultimately positive effects. They can be cunning or foolish or both. They rebel against authority, create convoluted schemes – that may or may not work - play with the Laws of the Universe (or the State of New York) and can be their own worst enemy.

Tricksters are creators, jokers, truth tellers, story tellers. Geisler and Roberdeau doubtless believed that out of their trickery would come great works of art . . . and *then* the people they owed money to would have their reward. Prometheus and Coyote stole fire from heaven – and that was good, wasn't it? But the strain of cancelling cheques and fighting off creditors must have been huge, because these people didn't understand the Trickster myth. The burden of it all – as well as the inexorable toils of litigation – may have killed John Roberdeau. The thin red line stopped suddenly, in the lobby of a hotel.

It's a tragic story.

I think of the 'maelstrom' of litigation which the wise Judge Sweet referred to. Of all the hatred, which caused John Roberdeau, in an interview, to call his former partner and generous investor 'a coward and a deserter', and Barry Goldin to refer to Roberdeau's 'purported death'. All absurd and destructive. What does it matter, in the face of love – and death?

Again

So you've come to me again,
My great love, my fury, my gypsy woman,
Thirty years of my life
And yours.

And what an arrival!
Seeing me in bed with your mother –
Though fortunately a space between us –
You ask if you should climb in,
And I say yes, of course.
Off comes your dress, and your thickened,
Beautiful hips and thighs of
Your maturity clamber in
Between your mother and me,
Those black stockings and suspenders,
And when you lie down by me, I stroke
Your thighs tenderly, desiringly.

We are in a group of serious-minded tourists;
I'm guiding them around the Ashmolean,
Where you and I went once,
You visiting my Oxford youth;
I point out to them, excitedly,
Some classical stones or bones
That are moving, rising, stirring.
They're astonished. Shall these
Bones live shall these bones live?

You're now youthful, slender and pretty,
My black haired gypsy girl,
As when I took you secretly to Ireland.
You murmur, with a sweet ironic curl
Of your lips, 'So you don't want to marry me?'
'Of course, of course!' It would be right,

On Goldin Pond

Since it's clear, despite your tan and juiciness,
You haven't long to live. It's right;
You're my great love,
I'm your great love. I feel
A little awkward introducing you
To the serious, sceptical tourists,
Being so much older . . . But it's okay.

Do the bones really live, my love?
The stones and bones move again and lift,
Reassuring me.

I'm back at a college – not the one
Where we met; I'm department head.
It's late at night. No one's there.
Then two lecturers arrive by car,
And spot me in the dark. I hear
One say, 'What's Thomas doing here
So late?' 'Oh, probably feathering
His nest,' the other replies, with a chuckle.

As I sat of an early evening
In my study, dusk falling,
Before driving home to my family,
I'd think of you in your dorm
Across the road from me,
The window-lights visible,
And ached to be able to see you;
Ached with jealousy
About who you might be meeting –
Like the SAS soldier
You told me about,
Who padded so light-footedly
Through Hereford.

Seven years after your death,
The seven year itch
To be with you again.
That's why you came.

Strenue ac Fideliter

Faced with the daunting task of getting finance and a director, in one year, Susan Potter/JOA Productions settled eventually on Philippe Mora, director of *Communion* and a host of other movies, as her director and co-producer. I'd never heard of him; but that wasn't unusual. When I met him, together with Susan and their spouses, in London in May 2005, I immediately took to him. Potter and Mora had just flown from Cannes, the Festival, where their project had been received with, they said, incredible enthusiasm. Juliette Binoche's agent had phoned them to say she would love to be considered for the movie.

Susan had produced, for Cannes, eye-catching promotional posters and postcards. They depicted a glamorous Lisa in a low-cut gown and a thoughtful cigar-holding Freud, together with a three-spired Gothic hotel. The text:

> 'JOA Productions presents . . . *A dream of electrifying eroticism and inexplicable violence.* From director Philippe Mora THE WHITE HOTEL. *Based on the award-winning novel by D. M. Thomas. Screenplay by Susan Potter.*'

I thought it rather impressive. A film seemed really close, especially with the news about Juliette Binoche. Her name would bring a major actor for Freud.

I was struck immediately by Philippe Mora's openness, intelligence, modesty and gentle humorousness. He had a passionate interest in Freud and the Nazi period. In his mid-fifties, he had not yet made a 'big' movie, and I sensed he felt this could be the one.

Mora was born in France, but spent much of his early life in Melbourne, Australia. I had spent those two memorable and seminal years there, in my teens, moving from 'Beano' comic to *Macbeth*. To our delight we found we had attended the same school, University High School. It was where I really started my intellectual development, and I have always been grateful to it. Mora and I sang the school song together, after a few glasses of wine, and recalled the school motto, *strenue ac fideliter*, 'with zeal and loyalty'. He promised to work with zeal and loyalty to make the film. I knew he meant it.

While he was in London, he was going to meet Juliette Binoche. Seen as a likely Lisa back in the Kusturica period, she was totally committed, they said. Mora interviewed me, using a video camera, so he could demonstrate to her how I felt about my novel. Philippe and I were already the best of friends when we parted.

Angela, an unpublished but richly talented Canadian novelist, was now with me in the Coach House. She had spent the last three years writing in solitude, first in Prince Edward Island, then in a French chateau. It wouldn't be easy for her to get used to living with me – and with an even greater age difference – thirty-four years – than between Victoria and me; but we chuckled at the same oddities, and felt hopeful we could make a go of it. She would first have to return to Canada to apply for an extended visa. It would have to be 'engagement' status. We loved each other, and wanted to live together; but – so soon after my divorce – we both felt it would have been better if we could have eased ourselves into the relationship gently, not under diktat from British Immigration. Effectively: marry within six months or she's out. It maddened me that Germans could walk into Britain, yet Canadians, who had fought and died beside us in two World Wars, could not. Beaumont Hamel, Vimy Ridge, Juno Beach – good God, did they mean nothing?

We had met several years earlier, at one of the Humber workshops. She'd spoken to me at the opening wine-and-cheese event. I'd said, 'I'm going outside to have a cigarette: do you smoke?'

She said, 'No, but I can start.' I liked that. She didn't start. A pity, I thought, she's dressed drably in trousers and wears no make-up, but an *interesting* face. I smoked on a grim concrete patio and we talked. I was aware of her intense focus, her obvious passion for writing. She wasn't in my workshop group; we didn't see each other again till the closing banquet, when we talked for a few minutes. We'd then, on my return home, carried on a long e-mail exchange, in which I poured out my grief and remorse over Denise. Angela's responses were always understanding and helpful. I told her my dreams, and found she had remarkable insight into them.

Now, in the spring of 2005, she was sharing my home. With the 'Goldin' frenzy behind me, and no longer being sued for $4.2 million, I felt a burden lift. I might even be able to write. Joyously, frenziedly, I gathered up all the mountainous rolls and scrolls of legal faxes, covering almost every surface, and stuffed them into black bin-bags. It felt sweet to have only books strewn around my study. With luck, I would never have to talk to another lawyer, ever.

Pushkin said that, for inspiration, calm is more important than ecstasy. He was right. And calm was beginning to come. Admittedly I had nothing in my head, no theme. I kept looking aside from my desk to a portrait of Anna Akhmatova, seeking her help. So similar in face to Denise, and sharing her June birthday, she was one aspect of the Muse. The Muse was still on her sabbatical. But with calm in my house and study, she might return.

FOUR

Cornwall – Hollywood

A Certain Momentum

Prospects were certainly starting to look good for the film. Binoche was 'rock-solid', Anthony Hopkins reportedly was very interested in playing Freud, and a financial package of $15 million was only awaiting someone's signature. Philippe kept me constantly in touch with exciting news . . .

> I'm planning to be back in London very soon for the film.
>
> Things are gung ho on the film and progressing quickly. We have a certain momentum. I like to say we have to turn the momentum into a perfect storm (a positive one). Then we shoot!
>
> Cheers
>
> Philippe

We usually signed off our e-mails with our old school motto, *strenue ac fideliter*, or some variation of it. His zeal and loyalty were unmistakable. Disappointments never fazed him. When news came from Susan that the expected huge financial deal had fallen through, Philippe was quick to reassure me . . .

> 01/07/05
>
> Hi Don: DO NOT BE DISCOURAGED AT ALL! That was always a long shot with that financial group.
>
> Without going into a blow by blow our strategy was always to cast Freud, Lisa and Lover/Soldier and then get the money. Why? Because the finance question ALWAYS no matter how great the material – and it is great – is WHO IS IN IT? Well, we are nearly there with the bankable answer (cast package) to that query . . .

My guess is we will get news about Hopkins on July 5th here – next Tuesday.

Then we will make some major moves either with him or without him. The fun is only just beginning.

Cheers

Strenuac Fideliter

Philippe

P.S. Of course there is always Illegitimi Non Carborundum – which I am led to believe means: Don't let the Bastards Grind You down!

26/07/05

Dear Don: It's looking very good for Hopkins to play Freud. Must be a Welsh thing.

Meanwhile FYI I found (below) this long, but sometimes really fascinating academic paper about Freud on screen.

Cheers

Philippe

His next e-mail brought news that made me feel that the film was now certain to be made . . .

30/7/05

Hi Don: Hopkins has agreed to play Freud. He has not signed yet, so mum's the word. There is still some negotiating to do with his agent.

Joely Richardson has agreed to play Vera. She is a personal friend, but that aside, she will be a terrific Vera. We are getting there.

Strenue ac fideliter (What is the correct spelling?)

Cheers

Philippe

Hi Philippe: I can't get a reply from Susan regarding Binoche and whether she has read her revisions. I hope the silence is not ominous. What news?

    Strenue,

    Don

Hi Don: I don't think she has read it yet. We would have heard through her agent or she would have e-mailed me directly. However, this is not ominous. She finished shooting a strenuous picture last week in London and started shooting a new picture in Paris this week. She has been flat chat since I met her and she told me she would be. The cold reality is positive: With Hopkins now agreeable, she is not indispensable to getting this done if she suddenly went south for whatever reason. I emphasize there is no indication of that at all. If she still has script issues after the revisions I'm sure she can be accommodated.

    Cheers

    Philippe

03/09/05

Dear Don: Just a heads up that I expect some action next week on The White Hotel on various fronts. Juliette Binoche e-mailed her LA agent this week that her "acting coach" read the rewrite and liked it. She is yet to read it, but in the arcane etiquette of all this, the message is very positive.

I think I may have mentioned to you that I took the liberty of showing her the interview we did together at the Pelham Hotel and she was very impressed.

America is reeling today from the biblical proportions of the catastrophe in New Orleans. It seems particularly tragic – if there is such a graph – that the home of the creation of jazz gets bashed up.

We are looking forward to a visit ASAP.

Cheers

Philippe

02/09/05

Dear Don: Binoche ciao (see her note) – too bad. I think casting is a Zen exercise.

We will make an offer to Kate Winslet today.

I am not concerned or as you may said as a kid in Melbourne – no worries.

Until very soon,

Philippe

22/09/05

Bit of a downer, Philippe. She might have made up her mind sooner; like, four months ago . . .

Don

Yes it is a bit bizarre, especially since she contacted us in the first place.

Onwards! We are moving with alacrity.

Cheers

Philippe

Going to the Pictures

I've never lost the feeling of tingling excitement on entering a darkened cinema, as I felt when I went with my father, after rugby, into Redruth's Regal Cinema. Most boys went to the Gem, just a street away, where the action pictures were shown – Tarzan and such like. But dad always took me to the Regal, where there were 'grown-up' pictures, with Bette Davis, Barbara Stanwyck, Spencer Tracy, Humphrey Bogart, Greer Garson and so on. Through these films, even at nine or ten, I had a glimpse of mature themes and emotions.

Or there'd be an Abbot and Costello on. Dad loved them,

whereas he didn't like Laurel and Hardy. As Costello stuttered and played the fool, dad's laughter would ring out, loud ascending arpeggios of hilarity, unmistakable, making everyone else laugh at his laugh; so that his workmates would say to him on the Monday, 'Heard 'ee in the Regal Saturday, Harold!'

Mum never went to the pictures. Her entertainment was going 'up Carnkie', her and dad's birthplace village (and mine too), for a cup of tea and a 'bit chat'.

When we emigrated in 1949 to Melbourne, Australia, the pictures preceded rather than followed the football (Australian Rules now, not rugby). Dad and I would catch the tram on Saturday morning into the city centre. My first tentative experience of classical music came in such musicals as *The Caruso Story*; I found pleasure in the operatic numbers scattered among the popular songs, which I also enjoyed. Then, one holiday I went on my own, and saw Jean Simmons and Donald Houston in *The Blue Lagoon*. When Jean thought Donald had drowned, and gazed with dread and a love just realised out at the deep blue ocean, a powerful actor's voice spoke the opening lines of John Donne's 'The Good Morrow' . . . 'I wonder by my troth what thou and I / Did till we loved . . . ' And I thrilled to it – the first poetry that had moved and excited me. I thought, So *this* is what poetry is! And even more profoundly, So *this* is what love is!

I bought – or my parents bought for me – 'Photoplay' every month, and I thrilled to the sweater-girls – Janet Leigh, who told an interviewer she wore a 38DD brassiere (if my memory serves me correctly), Ava Gardner, Jane Russell, Doris Day . . . Though Doris was also very much the girl-next-door, like June Allyson, whom I also adored. The seductress and the girl-next-door: they would remain potent opposites in my life. I loved Anne Baxter too; and even though in *All About Eve* she was obviously the villainess I still saw her as the film's heroine, rather than Bette Davis.

Back in England in 1951, living in a close-knit, chapel-centred, once-mining village, Carnkie, for the first time since I was a baby; homesick for Australia as I had previously been homesick for England. Aged sixteen, never been kissed; the King's Cinema, Camborne, on a Saturday afternoon. On my left, my Carnkie pal Ronald, pale faced mummy's boy. On my right, an empty seat; but then a girl came and sat there. In the dim light I could see she was attractive. A young version of Jean Simmons. The first sweet, intoxicating Woolworth's scent of a girl – close to me – closer – pressed against me. She asked if I had a light. (Those wondrous days, when people smoked in cinemas and – miraculously – no one around you coughed, no one threw up their arms in their death throes from asphyxia.) I told her I didn't smoke. She whispered there was a fair on, was I going to it after? My mind whirled like the Waltzers; I wanted to go with her so much; but there was Ronald . . . and mum would be expecting me back on the six o'clock bus . . . I said no, but would she meet me the next Saturday, at two, outside the cinema? She said yes.

After a week I spent in delirium, counting every minute, she didn't turn up – of course. I caught the bus into Redruth, thinking she might have meant the Regal. She wasn't anywhere. The first raging romantic disappointment, and the determination that I would never again let the moment pass. Carpe DM. Remorse would be better than regret.

Later, with Maureen, my first girlfriend, then fiancée, smooching in the back row. The triumph of a stocking top caressed. Not much later, aged nineteen, learning Russian at Cambridge during my National Service, alone in a small arts cinema I watched Marlene Dietrich vamp in black stockings and suspenders around a stage in *The Blue Angel* . . . and didn't know what to do with the throbbing erection in my trousers. I moved my position to try to get more comfortable – and ejaculated. I was drenched. And overwhelmed with excitement.

You could actually have an orgasm *deliberately*, I suddenly realised, not just in a wet dream. I spent the rest of that weekend masturbating in the toilets at our officer cadet lodge. Kinsey would have been shocked by my backwardness.

Yes, I owed a lot to the cinema, culturally, emotionally, sexually. And Hollywood was where my parents had spent their golden years, their twenties in the 1920s. My father, working as a fitter at 20th Century Fox, had proudly brought my mother and Lois, an American-born toddler, to see the studio; and she had been dandled on the lap of Walter Pigeon. The bungalow my father built in Redruth was called 'Beverly'; we had a Hollywood-style 'breakfast nook' and 'cooler'. Letters came in from his older brother, settled there. California was closer to us than London; and the American servicemen who courted Lois, and who brought dad cartons of Lucky Strikes and me chewing gum and baseball gear, brought it still closer.

Now, in my seventy first year, Philippe was making the magic real again, on this roller-coaster of a ride.

Off to the Races!

30/09/05

Dear Don: Hopkins has approved both Kate Winslet and Tilda Swinton. So we are making an offer to Winslet post haste.

LA is literally on fire – 25,000 acres burning – the sky is black and red in certain parts. Its either arson or biblical.

Until very soon – Cheers

Philippe

01/10/05

Hi Don: Swinton has read it and wants to do it but we await response first from Winslet – could take a week. Watson is great also. We are getting close.

Cheers

Philippe

18/10/05

Hi Don: Winslet has officially just passed. We have just informed Tilda's agent/s

(Endeavour also reps Gael Garcia Bernal – excellent and 'hot' for 'lover' – Tilda and Bernal are friends) and they are very happy. Now, assuming Tilda has not gone South/mad/ hit by a piano/ bitten by a rabid dog, etc, we are in excellent shape. We expect to get a quote for her by the end of the day, make the official offer – THEN WE ARE OFF TO THE RACES, MATE!

Strenuac

Cheers

Philippe

19/10/05

Great! Let me know if you hear from Tilda herself.

saf

Don

20/10/05

Hi Don: I had a great conversation with Tilda Swinton, who lives in Scotland. She said she held the Freud pillow in her performance work 9 years ago because she had read your book. She is very smart and will be a great Lisa I have no doubt. She greatly appreciated your message and will be in touch in due course as we proceed.

I need to get over to your neck of the woods soon.

Onwards!

strenuac

cheers

Philippe

An e-mail arrived from Susan Potter saying that Anthony Hopkins had pulled out. Again I wrote to Philippe to see what he made of this.

Cornwall – Hollywood

Cher Don: Actually, my initial response was The Fucking Shit! Shortly thereafter I went Zen and into action. Endeavour represents Bernal, Swinton and Hoffman. They are seized with this as we speak, for mercenary reasons as well as the fact that Binoche (their client) keep us waiting for four months. They have the offer and are forwarding the script to DH now. I think four million will in turn seize his attention and we will get a prompt response.

These actors saying yes, then no, is a real problem (not just for us obviously). One can litigate and people have successfully, but as an Australian lawyer once said to me about suing: If you win, you lose. And if you lose, you're fucked. Or something like that.

All in all I think a Jewish Freud may be better than a Celtic Freud. When Hopkins played a fat Nixon in "Nixon" it was an excellent performance but it was not Nixon.

We will not let this delay us.

More to come very soon I am sure.

Strenuac

Philippe

Hi Don: In the continuing blow by blow account: Hoffman's agents spoke to him last night and he was "excited" per them about playing Freud in THE WHITE HOTEL. He wanted to read or reread the book (a good sign), see my film COMMUNION and read the script. I sense a fast response. We may be off to the races again with a jockey who doesn't jump.

Cheers

strenuac

Philippe

Bleak Hotel

24/11/05

Hi Don: No news except that Hoffman has a keen interest in playing Freud per his agent here, is reading your book, script, etc.

His agent told me that two days before we offered it to him Hoffman said that John Malkovich told him he should play Freud. I guess any Freud since we had not offered yours to him yet! His agent is very keen he does this.

It is Thanksgiving here when things close down until Monday: Americans celebrate Columbus introducing take-away pizza to the US, and the fact that American Indians gave the pilgrims turkey for which they were rewarded by being wiped out.

Cheers

strenuac

Philippe

A week after receiving that hopeful e-mail, Angela and I got married. We told no one, not even our close families, just the couple of friends who were to be witnesses. I had done this too often to want to have another wedding party, presents, and so on. Feeling anxious and somnambulistic, after I'd put on my wedding suit I lay sprawled on our bed, in what Angela recalls as a crucifixion pose. In my head was the question, Would I again fuck up? Would that old companion to marriage, claustrophobia, spoil what was a good and loving relationship? Embarrassment mixed with anxiety at the registry office, as I knew the gushing female registrar must have been wondering what this radiant young woman was doing with an arthritic old guy.

I winced through the tritely phrased vows since, for me, such solemn vows should only be spoken before God – even if He didn't exist; and in the poetic, awesome language of Cranmer – even if, as in my only church wedding, to Maureen, I felt I would almost certainly break those vows. Sexually, that is; I've never thought the vows related only or even mainly to sexual fidelity – for either of us, since I've always felt that what's sauce for the gander is sauce for the goose.

After champagne and smoked salmon at our friends' house Angela and I drove with them for a weekend in Dorset, Hardy country. Someone who knew a thing or two about marriages going awry. Sharing the back seat of the car with us was our friends' huge lurcher. Leaning over from the boot, which barely contained his body, he licked our faces in turn. My anxiety gradually eased with the help of the lurcher and laughter, and we had a great weekend driving around the Hardy places, returning at early dusk each day to a roaring fire in a country inn.

Going off in a foursome – or fivesome if one includes Matti the amiable and gigantic lurcher – relieved the pressure. I didn't have to leave the bride, going out on my own for a walk to ease breathlessness, as I did on my first night with Maureen, in London en route to the Lake District. I wasn't cramped on a sofa bed in Denise's parents' living room, while she tensed during sex in case her father heard us, next door, and had one of his crazy spells. I didn't suffer the remorse and grief over Denise I felt when Victoria and I had our short honeymoon in Devon; though this time I felt some guilt over Victoria.

I could hear the ghostly Carnkie voices gossiping . . . *'Did 'ee hear about Donald Thomas, Harold and Amy's boy? On his fourth marriage.'*

'Sure 'nuff? He didn't seem to have no time for girls. Always had his head in a book.'

'Still waters, i'n a, you?'

9/12/05

Hi Don: The saga continues. Hoffman passed per Peter Rawley and his agent – 'he could not see a way of getting into the role'. Loved the book and no problem with me – just couldn't see it – who knows. We are regrouping tomorrow.

You mentioned Ralph Fiennes liked it some time – We'll get there – unfortunately this is par for the course, but we have access to everyone so we will move fast.

Strenuac

Cheers

Philippe

Matriachs

An analogy strikes me: the movie making business is like sex. Constant tumescence, detumescence, tumescence, and then again detumescence . . .

I still find it baffling that I didn't discover – by accident – how to masturbate till I was nineteen. I had raged with repressed sexuality in my mid-teens, in Melbourne; gazed hungrily at the Hollywood sweater-girls in *Photoplay* and in cinemas; experimented for some months, when alone, by trying on my sister's or mother's underwear and stockings, trapping my erection under a roll-on or corset; I had gone 'almost all the way' with Maureen, whom I'd met during a home leave from Cambridge . . . How could I possibly not know one could stroke one's penis and – hey presto!

Perhaps I was defending something. And maybe a passage I give to Freud, in his analysis of 'Frau Anna' (Lisa) gives a clue . . . 'There is a joking saying that "Love is a homesickness"; and whenever a man dreams of a place or a country and says to himself, while he is still dreaming: "This place is familiar to me, I've been here before," we may interpret the place as being his mother's genitals or her body. All who have . . . had the opportunity to read Frau Anna's journal have had that feeling: the 'white hotel' is known to them, it is the body of their mother. It is a place without sin, without our load of remorse . . . '

My own mother, I would guess, was virtually without sin.

She was a simple, wise, Christian woman, kind and generous to all. She wasn't burdened by an excessive and unruly sexual instinct; she preferred, as she and my father joked, a bar of chocolate. Before her hair greyed early, in her late thirties, she had Mary Pickford good looks and glamour, for all that she was a miner's daughter. She bottle-fed me; certainly was no Earth-mother.

I don't often dream of her; but I dream often of Carnkie, where she, my father and I were born, and which was always the emotional centre of our lives. We lived there after our return from Australia, in the house where both dad and I were born. Like most Celtic mining villages, in Wales or Cornwall, Carnkie was really matriarchal. It had been sweetened and chastened by a century of Methodism. Even physically, this small world was feminine – the row of miners' cottages sunk in the *droke* (Cornish for cleavage) between the twin breasts of Carn Brea and Bassett Carn. And further down, on the way to Redruth, the valley we called the coombe, or *cwm*, the cunt. True, the women were imprisoned in boned corsets and bloomers and long-line brassieres and petticoats, but they were freer in many ways than the men, who worked hard for their game of snooker of an evening or glass of beer. (Not in dad's case; he and his brothers never drank, under the influence of my strong-principled grandmother.) The men knew their place; and put the pay-packet on the kitchen table on Friday evening, then waited for their cigarettes-and-beer money to be doled out. There was no such thing as sexual politics; men and women fought a common battle against poverty and illnesses, and found a common solace in song, chapel and neighbourliness.

Sex, for most – and certainly for me – was the innocence of seeing the women fumble off a nylon stocking at a Sunday School social, in a frivolous game, to shrieks of laughter. (I use 'frivolous' here in the Geisler/Roberdeau sense, when describing Goldin's 'frivolous lawsuit': i.e. for us watching boys, 'momentous, stunning, all-absorbing'.) Well, some men had affairs, I'm sure – the black sheep – but it was part of human frailty, and the miscreants were known and tolerated, for the most part. Especially if they were generous and kind. *'Willie? Oh, he's a good old sort! Do anything for anybody!'*

Once I had got over my homesickness for Melbourne, I began to love the gentle life of the village. And of 'St Martin's Villa', which we shared with my ever-toiling Auntie Cecie, genteel arthritic Auntie Nellie, gentlemanly, serene, pipe-puffing Uncle Eddie, sorrowful grumpy Auntie Ethel (she'd lost husband and two beautiful daughters to TB), and my cousin Gerald. All up and down the village too there were other aunts and uncles, even though we were not related. It's the landscape I dream of and go back to in my imagination, it's my white hotel. Everyone knew I was different, I was 'clever' and 'always studying', and they respected that. I think I must have sublimated my sexuality in books, poetry especially. There were wonderful, lyrical afternoons among the bracken and rocks of Carn Brea, reading Keats and Shelley. I was still, when I wished to be, part of the tight community, as I've never been before or since. I played snooker every night at the Men's Institute, sang 'My Grandfather's Clock' in the concert party.

I was defending, I now believe, that innocent life – which of course was partly unreal.

My aunts and uncles, real and honorary, were ageing. I didn't realise it. With no mines working, not for many a decade, there were few children around. When my father died, in 1960, the heart went out of the village. A year later, Auntie Cecie died, of pneumonia and heartbreak over dad. And very quickly the village – the village as I had loved it – vanished. It was like a small holocaust.

Solomon in All His Glory

A happy interlude during these litigious years was seeing my first – and surely only – stage play produced. It drew heavily on my love of those Cornish people of my youth, and of course my sense of loss. Also my love of rugby.

One match-day, when I was about eleven, dad and I were sitting in the stand at the Redruth ground at the game's end, waiting for the crowds to leave. We were in no hurry; we must have known that the double feature at the Regal wasn't due to start for an hour or so. In any case in those days you could wander in and out when you pleased, and we would often be ushered in when the 'B' film was half over. Then, later, we'd watch the film again to the point where we'd already seen it. It was an early exercise for me in post-modernism.

When the rugby spectators had almost all left, my father pointed to an old man in a shabby raincoat standing behind the goal posts at the 'Hell Fire Corner' end. 'You see that man? That's Bert Solomon.' His tones were awed, as if speaking of a god. Solomon had been, in his time as a rugby player, a god to the Cornish; and in 1946, when I had that glimpse of him, he'd become mythic, like that other Cornish hero-god, Arthur.

There was a whole sacred gospel of stories about Bert. He was an uneducated, illiterate tin miner, and later pig butcher; tall, immensely strong, fast and elusive, he became the greatest centre-three-quarters that Cornwall, England, probably the world, and possibly the universe, had ever seen. He perfected the 'dummy', feinting to pass the ball to a fellow player but keeping it, so fooling his opponent. On one occasion the referee blew his whistle for an illegal forward pass from Solomon, who was touching the ball down across the score-line for a try. 'Forward pass! Scrum down!' 'But I never passed'n, ref; I still got the ball!' 'Oh, good lord, so you have, Solomon! Sorry! *Try!*' He was not a team-player, but independent-minded; and sometimes he'd opt out of a game because there was a carrier-pigeon race on. Then there'd be grief among the Redruth crowd. Grown men would weep (well, gospels can exaggerate). One story has a man arriving late at the ground, and telling his friend he has bad news for him – he'd glanced in at his front window and seen his missus cuddling up with another man. And the friend replies, 'And I've got bad news for you, my sonny – Bert isn't playing.'

The England team at the time consisted almost wholly of toffs, ex public school and Oxbridge men, officers and solicitors. The selectors ignored the illiterate Cornish miner for years; but at last they could resist no more, and picked him in 1910 to play against Wales at Twickenham. Solomon won the match with a delicious swerve around the Welsh full back. Then he went home by the milk-train overnight, eager to get back to his beloved pigeons. And declined to play for England again, though he was selected for the next two international matches. He felt out of place among the toffs; didn't know which knife and fork to use at the after-match dinner. Anyway, he'd made his point.

Over the years I've been haunted by Bert Solomon's story. We had attended the same elementary school, Trewirgie, in Redruth; our working-class backgrounds were similar. Born half a century later, I'd been able to go to Oxford; but even so I've never felt really comfortable with the 'toffs'. Metaphorically – and in early days even literally – I too don't know which knife and fork to use. I quite like feeling cut-off from the coteries of the *intelligentsia*; yet sometimes too I feel a wistfulness about it, and envious when reading about some author, suffering depression or hard times, who's been offered the use of an influential friend's villa in Tuscany or Provence. I've never been part of that privileged – and ironically almost always left-wing – circle. I felt and feel close to Bert. And for years wanted to write about him.

But how? A novel didn't seem the right *genre*. How to get

the roar of the crowd, the lilting dialect voices, the harmonic hymn-singing? – because I wanted it to be about the people too, their spirit and their hardship. For Cornwall, in Solomon's time, had lost a third of its population in the second half of the nineteenth century: forced by unemployment and poverty to vanish to mining camps in America, Australia, Canada, South Africa. Lung disease was rife among the miners; their average life span was about thirty. Women and children died as a result of hunger and poor housing. They needed King Arthur to return as he'd promised, and he came in the shape of another king, Solomon. 'Solomon in all his glory'. At last it struck me that I could only hope to express what I wished to express through a play or film script – and I'd had quite enough experience of trying to get a film made. A play it would be.

My first version had about sixty roles in it. Unsurprisingly, no one was interested. Then by chance I met a theatre director, Marie Macneill, who had just returned from London to her Cornish roots. She helped me to rewrite, using her skill and experience; we cut the number of characters to more reasonable proportion; and she persuaded the director of Cornwall's largest theatre, the Hall for Cornwall, to combine with her in mounting a production.

It was done, in April 2004, on a tight budget. Eight mostly youthful and inexperienced actors, partly chosen for being Cornish or having Cornish connections, who had never acted together; only three weeks' rehearsal in a Territorial army hall. They became three of the happiest weeks of my life: seeing my script take flesh, and feeling part of a common endeavour. For a short time, no longer the solitude of the writer's study.

The production of *Hell Fire Corner* ran for twelve performances. I was there almost every night; I thought, this is only going to happen to me once, I'm going to make the most of it. Marie's husband, John Macneill, brilliantly played the leading role, as a miner who worships Solomon. Audiences were quite small to begin with, but built up to a full house on the last night. People laughed and cried. A few local reviewers and theatre buffs said snootily it was an old-fashioned play; but a reviewer for the *Stage* referred to it as 'this mighty play', and I thought that was a mighty nice reaction. More importantly, hundreds came to see it who had never been to the theatre in their lives. People sometimes stop me in the street, or come up to me at a rugby match, to tell me how much they enjoyed it and were moved by it.

I wished my father could have seen it.

Scottish Queens and Welsh Dragons

04/01/06

Hi Don: I don't want to sound mysterious but things are looking good and there should be news on Friday. Meanwhile I am in touch with Tilda and she is still on board which is great considering Narnia has grossed more than 224 million dollars here.

Until later soon strenuac

Philippe

07/01/06

Hi Don: No news today re the casting of Freud. However, sorry to be pedantic about this but strictly confidentially Peter Rawley who is handling the matter with CAA is optimistic that we will get Hopkins after all and CAA wants him to do it. I can shoot him out in a shorter period and that has made a difference, along with Narnia I believe. He is still legally on the fence which is why we must stay stumm while this plays out.

Meanwhile it looks like I will be in Inverness on the 17th to meet Tilda Swinton. I'm firming up the plans now and will let you know.

This year is Freud's 150th something and the Austrians are celebrating that along with Mozarts 250th something. Ah, the smell of schnitzel in the air.

We are getting closer!

Cheers

Philippe

12/01/06

Is your Scottish trip still on? – Don

Hi Don: Yes – I am leaving on Sunday to meet Tilda, and I will call you from London or Inverness on Monday or Tuesday.

Hoffman has expressed interest again – I guess he heard about Hopkins thru the grapevine. Anyway Tilda (NARNIA – now a phenomenon) is key not either of them now. We do expect to hear from Hopkins shortly.

Cheers strenuac

Philippe

19/01/06

Hi Don: I had dinner with Tilda last night and will spend time with her today. She is terrific and committed – we are lucky.

I don't have your phone number with me – please e-mail it when you read this! I'll be in London tomorrow afternoon at Washington Mayfair hotel until 28th Jan. If I can get away I'd love to whirlwind visit you but let's see how it goes – I want to get this film locked down!

Rawley in London now talking to banks – always a good sign!

Hopkins passed – he can go fuck himself. I am thinking of Bruno Ganz for Freud and getting "names" for Soldier and Victor now.

Cheers

Golf View Hotel, Nairn

14/02/06

Hi Don: Summary: Tilda wanted too much control – out of proportion to her commercial cache.

Its a bizarre story which I will entertain you with in person.

Meanwhile we are very steady here and it looks like an Austrian group led by an old friend of mine may fund the lot as equity investment.

Until later very soon – my computer crashed which is why I have been out of touch.

Strenuac

Philippe

Hi Don: It's par for the course I am afraid. The only bizarre thing is that the 2 actresses who threw themselves at us ended up wasting our bloody time. I thought it was expedient to go with either of them because they were good and agreed to do it – at least per their agents. I am very hopeful that we can cast this quite quickly now that we are proactive.

I was told today that Naomi will get us an answer within a week. She has the script, looks forward to reading it and is in LA.

We will get this whole thing done.

Cheers and strenuac

Philippe

March 7 2006

Hi Philippe: No news?

strenue, Don

Hi Don: Oscars here delayed stuff – but action now: We are waiting on Naomi Watts re casting. Dustin Hoffman has come back again today expressing interest in playing Freud.

Cheers and strenuac

Philippe

Most directors would have kept the author ignorant of the frenetic shifts as they planned a movie; Mora never did. He granted me the courtesy of keeping me constantly informed. I appreciated that. I felt I was on the roller-coaster with him. The process – as well as being like sex – was like writing: Often I purr with self-satisfaction at the end of a day, reading through what I've written, then decide next morning it was crap. Luckily we writers can keep it to ourselves. I would have hated having Philippe e-mailing me every couple of days, asking 'How's the novel going?'

For every page that finds itself in a book, there are at least twenty in my rubbish bin. Of course it's the same process for actors, who may, for their own very good reasons, consider a role, think of accepting, change their minds, think again 'It could be interesting', but ultimately turn it down. It is absolutely no reflection on those admirable actors approached by Mora and Potter that they may have hesitated and finally decided this was not a movie for them.

I am also aware of the misunderstandings, even in the nuances of language, that may occur when phonecalls and emails fly between director, producer, actors' agents and the actors themselves, perhaps engrossed on a movie set. Binoche, Hopkins, Hoffman, Swinton, and all the others mentioned at one time or another by Mora and Potter would have their own small story to tell. Philippe and Susan told me the story from their own viewpoints – *strenue ac fideliter*.

FIVE

A Cast of Thousands

To Dream the Impossible Dream

I still like Bobby Geisler. If he rang the buzzer now, and I saw him standing outside, I would embrace him warmly.

I was finding out more about him and John Roberdeau all the time. Sean gave me *Gods and Monsters* by Peter Biskind (Bloomsbury 2005). It contained a fascinating essay on their relationship with Terrence Malick. Had I bought *Vanity Fair* of December 1998, where the essay first appeared, or had someone referred me to it, it would have explained a lot, much earlier. But I certainly hadn't been in the mood for glossy magazines in December '98, weeks after Denise's death.

I knew Bobby and John loved Malick's work and had invited him to direct *The White Hotel*. I knew they were thrilled when he eventually agreed to direct *The Thin Red Line* for them. What I didn't realise is the extent and duration of their obsession with him. They were far more involved with him, and their dreams of working with him, than with my novel. 'We were co-dependent,' Geisler said in an interview; 'I don't like to think this about myself, but we were members of a cult.' And Roberdeau added, 'We were the high priests of it.' Roberdeau, according to Biskind, had in his youth committed Malick's *Days of Heaven* to memory – every word, every shot, every cut. It's possible their mutual love for Malick's films brought Geisler and Roberdeau together.

Malick, the enigmatic recluse, for a time responded to them with warmth. When Roberdeau's brother developed leukaemia, Malick offered to donate his bone marrow. 'We behaved like family toward each other,' said Geisler. 'We liked each other, I thought, loved each other. He was the centre and circumference of our lives.'

All this was astounding to me. I'd thought the boys dreamed only of making *The White Hotel.* I thought they greeted each other every morning on waking with the softly-spoken words, 'The White Hotel!' It's like a woman who believes her lover has been besotted with her for twenty years, only to find he has been much more passionately in love with someone else. Except, in this case, I feel a mixture of amazement and amusement that I knew them so little. Their obsession with Malick may have been the reason why they did not make *The White Hotel* in the 1990s.

They tried desperately to draw him into directing something – anything – for them, but he was evasive. He wrote a screenplay of *The Thin Red Line*, but then stalled on it. So they seized on an idea he had of turning the Mizoguchi film *Sancho the Bailiff* into a stage play. They paid him $200,000, and plunged into expensive, meticulous, and somewhat precious research, as was their way. Everything from recording Japanese children speaking to plunging into ancient Japanese texts. Then they proposed setting up a six-week workshop, at the Brooklyn Academy of Music.

They took Malick to Warsaw to meet the distinguished director Andrzej Wajda, who had agreed to direct the workshop. Wajda had never heard of Malick, and criticised his script, saying it should be more Shakespearean. At the workshop, held in November 1993, the two temperamental artists fell out. More importantly for Geisler and Roberdeau, their investors – notably Rubin – *pulled* out. Geisler and Roberdeau had assembled a world-class company, for a mere workshop. Possibly the most expensive workshop in history: it ultimately cost $800,000. The result was a crowd of angry, unpaid people. 'The boys' had to sell their books, records, furniture. Geisler spent a night in the cells, charged with grand larceny: a charge later dismissed. He'd spoken of this to me in Paris, saying he'd passed the night using his cellphone to call drug dealers and girlfriends on behalf of others under arrest.

He and Roberdeau were evicted from their Greenwich Village home in 1996. Thereafter they lived in hotels.

They had only themselves to blame, for ludicrous excess. They chose to blame Rubin. They were brought down by love – love of a movie director.

Nevertheless, they did bring Malick to direct *The Thin Red Line*. They persuaded Mike Medavoy, head of Phoenix Pictures, to finance it. The film, produced by Robert Geisler, John Roberdeau and George Stevens Jr. (brought in by Medavoy) earned seven Oscar nominations. When I saw 'the boys' in New York in February 1998, I congratulated them on their great achievement; and was puzzled why shadows crossed their faces. In fact, Malick turned against them, and they had no hands-on part in the production. They were not allowed to set foot on the set, which was in Queensland, Australia. Medavoy, in a lawsuit in Los Angeles brought against him by Rubin, described the pair in court (to Barry Goldin no less) as 'a bunch of charlatans'.

Malick said he wouldn't go to the Oscars if they attended. Phoenix and Twentieth Century Fox threatened to remove their names from the credits if they accepted the Academy's invitation. They agreed not to go; but then decided to go anyway. They'd been sent tickets for the middle of a row, near the back, making it almost impossible for them to make it to the podium. Geisler booked a limousine and had his tuxedo fitted. The limo was on its way to fetch them when they decided not to attend after all. And Malick didn't show up either.

What hurt Geisler and Roberdeau most was the break with Malick. Geisler, as he counted out and swallowed seventeen pills, described to Biskind how the broken friendship had affected him: 'Several years ago, I didn't take anything. My face has started falling off. High blood pressure, diabetes, I got fat, I drink too much. I'm never going to get over this.'

It was the end, in acrimony, of a supercharged emotional threesome – though no doubt Malick himself never saw it in that way, and may have felt a need to break free. Within a few years Roberdeau would die, and Geisler would be alone. It's difficult not to feel compassion. At least, unless you are one of their creditors.

All Geisler and Roberdeau got out of the *Thin Red Line* experience was their nominal credit as producers – and $1.5 million from Medavoy; which – according to the 1999 court judgement against them – they proceeded to move from account to account, among their numerous different companies, and to a bank in London. It would seem they were determined nothing should go to Rubin, who in their view had let them down over the *Sancho* workshop. Goldin told a reporter from *Daily Variety* in February 2000 that Rubin had been almost broken by their constant demands for money. 'He had been saving his last bit of cash for a wedding gift to his daughter. Somehow they found out and insisted he spend that money on them.'

Roberdeau countered, 'His "Oh, I was broke!" story is just horse shit. The guy knew exactly what he was doing, and when he decided to quit he assumed he would never see another nickel. To me, Gerry Rubin is a coward and a deserter.' This of the man who for years had invested millions in financing their projects. And after that, of course, came the 'maelstrom'.

Tales of Hoffman

March 17 2006

Hi Don: Looks like we will be in London May 2nd then on to Cannes May 16th. Pamela and I will be at the Soho Hotel. Susan and Gabe at the '41' Hotel. All still on track financially. Casting, we await Hoffman. But not for long. The agent said he would do it for 6 million but that is too much. We offered less. Next film I do will be with puppets!

Cheers

Philippe

A Cast of Thousands

My mother's simple phrases come into my mind a lot: 'The Lord will provide' . . . . 'Play with your playmates' . . . 'It is more blessed to give than to receive' . . . 'What's to be will be' . . . 'Count your blessings . . . '

On her birthday, March 23, came ecstatic news from Mora. I could hardly believe it, so decided to seek confirmation from Potter . . .

Hi Susan, have I read Philippe's latest correctly – Hoffman has agreed to play Freud?

Yours, Don

Hi dear Don!! YES. Isn't that remarkable. We did not approach him for round 2, btw. We got the word re: Hopkins passing, and then mulled a few names over . . . Liam Neeson, for instance . . . not getting excited about anyone. Then a couple of weeks after that Hoffman's agent called and said he'd changed his mind and wanted to do the picture, and was asking $6mil. We spent a week crunching the numbers . . . and wondering how true this all was; wondering how to afford him. Then another call, and another . . . asking where our offer was. That's when they said, Look, he'll do it for $5 mil. The only proviso is that he meet with the director and the writer prior to shooting, to discuss the script. HOW FUN that will be . . . and we are loving it, of course.

Anyway, this means that we will not be able to cast a big star for Lisa . . . and what a relief that is . . . because names like Hilary Swank come up . . . and I don't think she's right at all. Too American. I try not to argue and silently hope for better. Turns out she's $6mil, too. So, hooray! We now are first thinking of Audrey Tautou – who is starring opposite Tom Hanks in The Da Vinci Code – see attached picture – film opens in May. She looks older now and is a good actress. My next pick is Franka Potente, who is 31, starred in Run Lola Run, and The Bourne Identity and The Bourne

Supremacy. Excellent actress, German, fearless, oddly pretty (Her pic too is attached).

We are waiting for Dustin to phone Philippe . . . which the agents said will be this week, as he's starting a new picture in NY on Monday, I believe. Then the final back and forth re: his terms . . . our countering. Then everyone signs.

Cheers,

Susan

Wow, it's 'Dustin' now!

But it was back to 'Hoffman' in her next e-mail. Hoffman, she wrote, had a friend whose favourite movie was Mora's *Mad Dog Morgan*; and he (Hoffman) wanted to watch that movie before committing finally. She hoped she and Philippe weren't being jerked around by his agents. 'Stay tuned. Stay prayerful . . . '

Goldin, on Rubin's behalf, was still suing Geisler – rumoured to be penniless and not knowing where his next meal was coming from – in New York, and at the same time suing *The Thin Red Line* people in Los Angeles. The man was a magician, in two or three places at once. The Svengali of litigation. He had granted Susan a three month extension, and appeared, she said, satisfied with the progress they'd made.

Hi Don: Looks like we will shoot in Prague with Gatteo Studios who have given us a good quote for below the line. Maybe a few days in Vienna – possible chance of shooting Budapest but I am waiting on that budget. Big advantage of those 2 cities is they have so many similar locations, ambience, faces, etc, to Vienna – makes my life easier. Earliest start is mid July – probably August. Depends how fast the banking agreements, etc., and contracts go – but should go fast, *all parties are motivated.*

Cheers

Philippe

A Cast of Thousands

G'day, bonjour: We made offers on Friday to Jeremy Irons for Freud and Hilary 2 Oscar Swank for Lisa. They are both at CAA and we got a sympatico hearing. CAA is very familiar with the project, and Peter Rawley has excellent personal connections over there. They know we are in a hurry.

As for Mr. Focker, I am reminded of the lyrics to the Beatles' Hello, Goodbye. They seem to fit the whole incident with him, or non incident.

With warmest regards,

Strenuac fideliter (I'll get this spelling right some day!)

Cheers,

Philippe

Hi Don: We ARE coming your way. We leave a week from Sunday – May 7, arriving in London on May 8. We shall go to Cannes on May 16–28. Pushing sales at that time. We are presuming that we shall, indeed, have a cast by then. With a firm start date – now mid-August – and money to flow! (without which one can't have a firm start date) . . . we have more leverage in terms of getting the actors to say YES or no in shorter time than the ongoing, loosey goosey type negotiations/hurry up and wait shit we experienced with the prima donnas: Hopkins and Hoffman. Hoffman would have broken the ever-loving bank with his over the top fee demands. So, we've submitted a firm offer to Jeremy Irons. Who I love. Asked for a May 1 response. On Monday, we heard he is reading the script. P. has asked for a meeting while we're in London.

We're now also in receipt of a PASS from Hilary Swank . . . who I thought was wrong, anyway. She responded very quickly. Thank you, Jesus! Then Philippe learned that Milla Jojovich (formerly Joan of Arc, Resident Evil chick, The Claim, and 5th Element) commands very high advances on presales. Very important. She's huge in the world, as it happens. And, it turns out that she's Ukrainian . . . and I can imagine her as an opera singer. We've asked for a quick response, pushing for next week . . . as we are telling the agent that we're leaving the country and would like to meet with her in LA, where she lives, prior to our departure. Push push, we hope, does the trick.

Do you think you and Angela would like to come up to London for a day/night. DO let us know. We'd love to see you – celebrate the FINALLY HAPPENING phase of this long journey. Celebrate your brilliant novel. Celebrate YOU!

Cheers, dahlink . . .

Susan

So I could add Hilary Swank and Milla Jojovich to the long list of fine actresses who have been, however briefly, Lisa Erdman. And Jeremy Irons to the long list of Freuds. Susan also said there might be a chance of getting Meryl Streep to play Aunt Magda. No longer Lisa, but her aged aunt . . .

Commitments

I went on a holiday trip that turned out not to be what I had expected. One of those holidays where you think, Oh god, there are five, no six, days still to go . . .

One night it was very stuffy and claustrophobic in my room, so I went outside for some fresh air. And there, to my amazement, was Denise! At last, when I'd almost given up on ever seeing her again. I was shocked by her appearance; her hair was greying, and fluffed out at the sides, totally unlike her. Her face looked serious and plain. Then I thought, it's been a long time since we met, of course she will have changed. She might have just come back from the Gulag Archipelago.

I had to steel myself to find out if she was still mine. I

thought of that Pushkin love poem where he says to a dead mistress, 'Only, longing, I want to say, I still love you, I am still yours: come here, come here! . . . ' I said, nervously, 'Are you – are you with anyone these days?'

At last there was an expression I could recognise, and a soft smile as she breathed out smoke from her Rothman and murmured: 'I'm not committed to anyone, if that's what you mean!'

Such a relief! I thought, that probably means she's had relationships, had sex, but nothing serious. Well, I've done the same. I said, 'That's good! I'm going to get a divorce and marry you!'

But after turning up like that, she disappeared again. My mother tells me she's found a way to allow me to live with Denise: St Martin's Villa, our old family home, where mum is living with my father, can easily be split into three: one part for her, one for dad, and one where Denise and I can live. I am puzzled how a two-storey house can 'easily' be split into three. Each 'flat' with a kitchen, a bathroom, etc.? Besides , my father would get depressed, living on his own. I see him slumped in an armchair, sad-looking.

And anyway, I don't know how to find Denise. All I know is, she's somewhere in London. I drive around the myriad London streets, desperate to find her. Everywhere I'm met by obstructions – dead ends, red traffic lights, road ups . . . It's an impossible mission. I have to get to my school to take my class in morning assembly. I'll search again this afternoon.

At school, I start the assembly. I've coached my class in a presentation, involving poems, pictures, readings from the Bible, and so on. They're making heavy weather of it; I am too. My mind isn't on my job. The assembly drags on and on. Everything goes awry.

And now I notice, on a classroom shelf, a neat pile of tattered old magazines. I recognise them, and my heart skips a beat.

They're my little collection of *Relate*, a soft-porn monthly of the early '70s, to which I subscribed. *Reader's Wives*. Amateurish black-and-white photos of them, together with appreciative letters. The mags should be at the back of my wardrobe, but my puritanical Head of Department has found them somehow – and placed them on the shelf here so I'll know my wickedness has been exposed. He always suspected I was a rake.

God, I'm for it when this is over!

Mrs E. T.

Relate showed naked breasts and pubic hair, and occasionally erect penises, but never sexual activity. The letters, from men and women, seemed to be genuine and highly-charged. One of the stars, perhaps the brightest, of *Relate* was a woman called Mrs E.T. I don't imagine Spielberg named his extraterrestrial after her, because Mrs E. T. was totally of this earth and earthy. In her fifties or sixties, plain, stout and peroxided, she was a primitive Earth Mother fast forwarded to the 1970s; or perhaps ten or twenty years earlier since, like most of the the wives in 'Relate', she wore already-superseded stockings and foundation garments. The charm of these women was that they were real, unglamorous – not the girl next door but the auntie next door. In her standing poses, she seemed almost about to take root in the ground. She exuded sexual confidence, and that came through as real attractiveness.

The adoring compliments she received, in the 'readers' letters', were expressed in terms which would have women today reaching for the bottle of suicidal sleeping pills or castrating razor blade . . . 'My darling Mrs E. T., your latest photos sent me in ecstasies, as always. I especially loved the one which shows your superbly pendulous breasts, drooping almost to your navel. Oh, what I would do to straddle over you and take the weight of those glorious teats in my hands! I adore also the way your suspender belt is almost hidden in the fleshy folds of your tummy, not to mention your heavy thighs, which your hubby is fortunate enough to be able to go between nightly, entering your divine haven . . . Thank you, thank you, my dearest Mrs E. T.'

She knew that 'pendulous', 'drooping', fleshy folds', 'heavy thighs' weren't insults, they were expressing grateful respect and love. She always responded with reciprocal gratitude . . . 'Dear Editor, I would like to thank W. H., Surrey, Jack and R. H., Herts. for their very kind letters in Vol. 5 no. 10, and I am very pleased that they get so much pleasure from my pictures. I enjoy very much displaying myself for all your male readers and will be happy to do so as long as they find my photos exciting. I enclose a rear pose as requested by Mr G. M., and hope he continues to enjoy himself with my pictures.

A special thank you to you Editor, for publishing my photos and readers letters, as I was wondering whether my time had run out.

Yours gratefully & sincerely,
Mrs E. T., London.

Her time must have run out by now. She enjoyed it while she had it. 'The grave's a fine and private place, / But none I think do there embrace.' Unless she's incredibly old, Mrs E. T. has gone into the stockingless, ungirdled dark.

Relate and its rather innocent brethren were swept away in the tide of hard, unemotional pornography. Swept away also was the male expression of an almost religious adoration of real unglamourised women. That adoration exists in plenty, as Nancy Friday found, rather to her surprise, when gathering male fantasies for her book *Men in Love*. But with feminism it went underground; the delicate courtesies of male-female discourse became as old hat as the trilby which Trevor Howard raised to Celia Johnson in *Brief Encounter*. One may imagine what Andrea Dworkin and Germaine Greer would have said to Mr C. H., Oxford, and Mr G. M., Lancs. As if in response, men created an infantilized image of woman, unthreatening and unreal: a Barbie Doll, thin, with huge undrooping breasts and (increasingly depilated) vulva gaping.

Mrs E. T. and her admirers seem stranger now than Spielberg's visitor from outer space. Women and men grew more alike – and more estranged. In the final words of *Love's Labour's Lost*: 'You, that way; we, this way.'

An Old Magazine

I sometimes wrote for such mags as 'Relate' myself: soft-porn pieces, under a pseudonym. They were easy and quite enjoyable to write, and the money was good. Denise occasionally helped me. We'd use the money to go on holiday.

I had a weird experience a year or so after her death, and wrote a poem about it . . .

Rubbing Against You

Browsing an old soft-porn magazine
that came to light in a garage drawer,
I start to read an unusually literate
'intimate confession'; at last recognising
the anonymous interviewer
is me: I'm electrified to read words
you spoke to me two decades ago,
in your flat, in bed, smoking,
earning us some money
that would take us part way to Venice.

Your erotic adventure with the young teacher
I remember: how you undressed each other

A Cast of Thousands

one night during a school trip
when your pupils were safely in bed;
how he felt he was floating;

but I didn't remember
how you weren't averse to a bit of frottage,
when you were hot . . . the rather attractive man
pressed up against you in the bus,
pretending to read his paper
but really rubbing himself against you.
How you 'pretended to sway with the bus',
but were 'really playing up to him.
I must have been really hot
because I had an orgasm.'

Unquenchable desire and torment
as I frot against my fingers.
I want to ask more questions:
'Did he know you were aware of him frotting?'
'Did he come, as he read his paper?'
'Do you think he knew you orgasmed?'
Even dead, you turn me on like crazy. I'm
that man, stepping dazed from the bus,
walking on air, my crotch soaked and not caring.

SIX

We Rock, We Roll

Czechs and Cheques

I dreamed I was in love with someone but I don't know who. I don't think it was Denise. I miss her. Where is she? Does she come less often because she knows I am with Angela? It was harder for her with Victoria here, because our relationship started before we knew Denise was ill; she only knew she was always tired and had a very painful shoulder and neck, I only knew she would not have sex and I felt resentful. One of those vicious circles. An idiot doctor ascribed her pain to the menopause, treated her with painkillers, and eventually sent her for physiotherapy. The physiotherapist refused to treat her until she'd had an x ray; which showed a vertebra almost eaten through by cancer. If she'd had physio she would probably have become quadriplegic during her last two years of life. But equally if we'd had sex – as she later told me.

She had to have a kind of helmet drilled into her skull, until her neck could be operated on. So brave, she told the surgeon, before she went under to have the helmet fitted, 'Well, it will be harder to find men who are turned on by a helmet than stockings and suspenders!'

She is around. Just not showing herself. Only through the garden she made.

May 11

Lovely Don . . . All is going VERY well, and if they continue, which we are all working diligently toward . . . we should have some checks to write to you, among others, before we leave for Prague on June 2. We should be there in time and on budget. BTW, we're smoking all over the Charlotte St.

Hotel. They've even supplied ashtrays when they saw we were using saucers and cotton swab jars. SEE!

Ask and you shall receive. Talk soon.

XXX Susan

Her reference to writing checks was very welcome. My Agreement with JOA, her company, had been for an up-front payment on signature (Dec 04) of $25,000, with the same sum payable in February 2005. The first payment arrived five months late; the second still hadn't come, fifteen months past the due date. At first I had pressed her for it almost every week, and she was always 'about to' be able to pay me: just waiting on two upright, honourable investors from Oregon who were daily, hourly, for months, going to transfer $6 million to her. But later I gave up. It was hard to sound money-conscious with someone who was constantly invoking Jesus. I knew she intended to pay me one day, but other debts were more pressing; I was on the back burner. I had no hold on her. As she wrote back once, in a rare bad humour, 'What are you going to do – SUE me?'

Basically she had no money. She told me a member of her church had lent her enough to finance the May 2005 trip to Cannes and London, and pay me the overdue first payment. She and her husband Gabe didn't own their home, or even their car. 'She ate the air, promise-cramm'd'. And so did I.

But now – 'some checks'!

05/17/06

Hi Don: Just arrived in Cannes a couple of hours ago – Prague fantastic – found the White Hotel! – will send pictures.

Inches away from proper finance closing – a lot of paper to be done! All gung ho!

More soon – just unpacking suitcase.

Cheers

s f

Philippe

May 29

Hi Don . . . We are all so looking forward to seeing you tomorrow night. The Czechs found for us the white hotel par excellence. I'm sure Philippe will be showing you the pictures and video he took while in Prague and the nearby Chateau Ploskovich, which he found on May 11 and 12. I've attached a couple of pictures for you to get a preview. It's like they read your book and my script and went out and built it specially for us!! (At least this is what I imagined.)

Just so you know we are still trying to cast this picture. But the money deal is moving forward . . . if not at a pace . . . steadily and surely. We are now just waiting to hear re: our latest offers to actors. The goal is to be shooting by Sept 1st. God willing.

Cheers,

Susan

From the phrase 'steadily and surely' I gathered, Czechs but no cheques.

Wine and Ice

As your birthday approach – you would have been sixty one – I willed myself to dream of you, and an image of you came; but it wasn't you; it was forced, like a poem one writes because inspiration has disappeared.

So, in your absence, let me remind you of a previous reunion, shortly after Ross was born. It was the only time I'd left you, foolishly thinking I could do without you. The thought of having a second family, while I was still living with my first, unnerved me. And there was that very attractive, bright blonde from North Wales I'd met at a writing workshop. So I went. It was of course cruel to you, so close to the birth, and I'm sorry.

But after a few weeks of driving to North Wales every week-end, I was longing to see you again, and to see my just-born son. I phoned you, and you said alright, come round. It was an icy January evening as I drove to the estate where you had a little rented house. I parked and walked to your door, nursing a bottle of wine in my arms. I slipped on the ice and the bottle smashed. You were opening the door, and laughed. I laughed too and, seeing you, suddenly felt – home. Second home, anyway.

You showed me Ross asleep; then we went to bed and made love. And you told me you too hadn't been an angel – and why should you have been, since I still lived, as friends, with Maureen? And I was crazy with jealousy, but also curious and excited and wanted you to tell me everything; and you did; and then we made love again.

And since that day we didn't part. It took death to tear us apart; and even that isn't enough. We haven't said everything. We will never have said everything.

Christ Walking on the Waters

Our rendezvous with Susan and Gabe Potter, and Philippe and Pamela Mora, at the Charlotte Street Hotel, London, turned out to be not quite the triumphal celebration Susan had anticipated. They'd come to Europe expecting to stay for six months, through the preparation for and making of the movie – but unfortunately the money had not turned up. A wealthy German, Horst Danning, whom Mora had persuaded to finance the movie to the tune of $25 million, had suffered a fall in his home, and knew nothing more till he came round in intensive care at the Los Angeles Cedars-Sinai Hospital. He would have to recover before he could be asked to sign the document.

There were other problems, just coming to light. The

Danning investment depended on Philippe's obtaining a Letter of Credit from the Bank of Ireland. Mora and Potter had assumed this would now be straightforward, but it wasn't. Where was the Cast, where were the stars which could justify such a large budget? Well, there weren't any, yet. Philippe said there soon would be, they weren't going to be making *The Invisible Man*! But with a sinking heart Susan realised they were in no position to move to Prague for pre-production. Both couples were going to have to return to the States, to wait. For Danning, and for the Letter of Credit. And for actors. It had been a very expensive 'move to Europe'.

Yet Susan, at our first meeting in the hotel's library, was in tremendous, vatic form. She was no longer Peaseblossom or Mustardseed, but like some dramatic Ukrainian holy woman. Her quiet husband, Gabe, chewed a cigar and watched her with a look of adoration. She gave a wonderfully simple and true description of what *The White Hotel* is about: 'a woman trying to get well'.

'If Christ could walk on the waters,' Susan exclaimed, her eyes blazing, 'we can make this movie! If He could raise the dead, we can make this movie! And we will! I'm in the mood for miracles! When we arrived and found there was no money, we went to Westminster Abbey. And we heard, in the sermon, "I am the vine, you are the branches", and I immediately felt calm and certain again. I'm like the retarded little child in the TV show, who never gives up! Just now I was lying down in our room, listening to opera on my Ipod, and it was so wonderful that I cried; and I said to Gabe, I just want to make great art!'

A pause, while a waiter served us vodka tonics; then again: 'Goldin is very pregnant with it. He is very pregnant with me. My soul is pure.'

'Why aren't you mad?' I asked. 'Why hasn't this driven you mad?'

'Because of Jesus.'

It was time to go out to dinner. This was to have been the great celebration dinner – celebrating the final phase of the long journey and my 'wonderful novel'. She'd asked if we preferred French or Italian. Either would be fine, I'd responded. But I hadn't anticipated a *pizzeria*. And of course Susan couldn't have known that I loathe cheese. What was just as disconcerting was that they didn't seem to mind too much whether the Moras found us or not. They were out shopping, Susan said airily; and they wouldn't like where we were eating. Only when we offered to ring their cellphone did Susan use her own phone to call them. It didn't seem to occur to the Potters that we were as eager to see Philippe and his elegant, sultrily beautiful wife Pamela, as them. The Moras eventually arrived, and everyone ordered.

It was refreshing, Susan said, to eat pizza and pasta after the surfeit of oversauced meals they'd all eaten in Cannes. Well, certainly cheaper; and it was clear that money – the money the Potters had raised from investors for the expensive trip – was getting tight. Our table rained Parmesan. I had chosen the only non-cheese dish on the menu, a vegetable soup, but there was such a rain of sliced Parmesan descending from graters that I still got some of it in my soup. Not a rainfall, a snowfall. To parody Joyce, snow fell on the silent table, cheese falling softly, softly falling, on all the living and all the dead.

There was sniping between the couples. They'd already spent nearly a whole unproductive though luxurious month with each other, in London and Cannes. That's hard. Even Christ's disciples must occasionally have sniped. '*Shaddup!*' '*Don't you tell me to shaddup!*' Mostly the sniping was between Gabe and Pamela, as they leapt to the defence of their respective spouses. A dispute over money, I picked up in the background: who was taking advantage of whom. Their conversation grated, just like the hovering cheese-bearing waiters. The celebration dinner ended with Gabe, embarrassed, finding his credit card not being accepted because of some technicality, and having to go outside to phone his bank and sort it out.

Susan was never less than warm-hearted and hospitable to us. I could sympathise with her plight. When they'd set off from LA with their daughter – who had been seriously ill – and the Moras for Europe, she'd assumed there'd be $25 million in the account, thoroughly justifying first-class air fares for everyone and first-class hotels in Cannes, London and Prague. Hearing from Philippe the horrid news of Danning's plight and the stalled Letter of Credit must have been traumatic. Then, I feel sure they must have been embarrassed at having to entertain us a little less lavishly than they had hoped and intended, simply because the money had run out.

The Moras took us to their bedroom at the end of the evening to show us slides of the splendid set, a former royal chateau, they had found in Prague. They also unloaded some of their feelings about the Potters. 'They're amateurs!' Pamela exclaimed. And Philippe added, 'Calling on Jesus and miracles in serious meetings with potential investors! Christ!'

Angela and I moved to another, less expensive hotel next day, paying for ourselves. We all went to the theatre in the evening, to see Jeremy Irons, another distinguished not-player of Freud, in a rather tedious play. After, we found a Chinese restaurant, where the food was excellent and cheap. At one point Susan and Gabe got up almost as one to go to the restrooms. We mused aloud that they might have gone for a quick bonk. They returned together and, as he sat, Gabe growled, 'I suggest we all pay for our own meals, okay?'

It all felt uncomfortable. The best moment of our trip to London was seeing my month-old granddaughter, Lucy Lamorna Houston, Sean's first offspring. He looked very proud and tired. Till this point, he's led a carefree bachelor life.

After the return of the Potters and Moras to California, I e-mailed urging calm and reconciliation, for the sake of the project. Susan responded that she and Philippe had had a good one-day trip to Prague, between London and home. They were now offering the role of Lisa to Monica Bellucci. I thoroughly approved the choice of her to not-play in *The White Hotel*. I e-mailed a request that her contract give me *jus primae noctis*. They were still within an inch of getting the $25 million, but Horst Danning was still in intensive care. Susan was urging Philippe to go to the hospital and at least talk to Danning's lawyer; but Philippe said firmly that he would wait for Horst to be on the road to recovery.

01/07/06
Hi Don: I just got a fax from Susan Potter's lawyer saying I am terminated as director/producer of the film.
　　Strenuac,
　　Philippe

Susan: What the fuck is going on?
　　I knew there were tensions but – christ! so near to getting the $25 million! I don't understand. Please e-mail.
　　Don

In response, she complained that Philippe's dismissal was confidential and he shouldn't have told me. It was the first time I'd heard that a man who'd been sacked had a duty to keep quiet about it. There had been, she said, 'recriminations and accusations'. She had lost faith in his ability to land the 'big money fish' and attract a cast. She'd now got an extension from Goldin till September 8, and believed that was ample time for her to find money and start production in Prague on October 23. I loved the confident precision of the date. She had been having talks with a new, unnamed director, eager to oblige, who she believed would help her pull it off.

According to Philippe, she had been 'basically incommunicado' since he had queried an expenses invoice she had sent to him in May 2006, when he was trying to close the financial deal. The invoice was for $1.5 million. Philippe told her the investor and bond company would find the amount unacceptable.

He had misunderstood the invoice, Susan told me; it recorded not only what she had spent but all the loans she would have to pay back; if he had called her she could have explained, but he did not.

Whoever was incommunicado, it was clearly Mora who was suddenly, via a lawyer's letter, *excommunicado*.

In large part, I think, they were both victims of circumstance. With only a one-year option guaranteed by the JOA/Goldin contract, pressure was constant. There was also the millstone of Goldin-Rubin's totally unrealistic demand for a return of $3 million for his client. $25 million was too much equity for a film without big stars – as increasingly seemed likely – yet a small budget movie wouldn't have been able to raise the $3 million pay-off. Another option deadline was fast approaching. As in a marriage of opposites – Potter flamboyant and theatrical, Mora the quiet movie pro – mutual irritation grew as the road got rockier. Again as in marriage, money was a cause of discontent. The happy foursome that had set off for London, Cannes and Prague, anticipating money aplenty, had grown fractious when it failed to appear: with Susan and Gabe wondering why Philippe always needed to come with Pamela. Yet if Potter came with her husband, why shouldn't Mora come with his wife?

Everyone who's been in a bickering marriage has had the experience of a remark or tone of voice being misunderstood. Or that he or she can sincerely believe was misunderstood. So it was with the Potter-Mora relationship. On one occasion in London, Potter said ' Aren't you clever!' to a young female lawyer she'd just met, who was trying to help them with the finances. Mora saw the remark as condescending; Potter protested that she had meant it sincerely.

Now she had shown an unexpected ruthless streak. I hoped she wouldn't come to regret this peremptory, Islamic-style divorce. The possible Danning millions were lost to her; a few months later, recovered, Danning would be working with Mora on a film about Salvador Dali. Mora believed she had 'snatched defeat from the jaws of victory', and she only had to 'do very little', just not interfere, while he organised everything. Potter naturally disagreed, pointing to the absence of star actors, and saying he wouldn't have got his Letter of Credit, and therefore nothing from Danning, unless and until stars were attached.

This parting of the ways, Susan wrote, was 'not the end of the world but the beginning of a new life'. She only wanted to 'honor my trust' in her. I responded that, since this was a new life, she might start by paying me the long-overdue $25,000. Sticking to a contract was the best way of honouring trust, I told her.

I felt desperately sorry for Philippe. True, he'd been over-optimistic about landing stars, but he'd worked his balls off for this project – strenuously and faithfully, as far as I was concerned. I would greatly miss the warm human contact. I wrote to tell him so, and that I hoped we'd always be friends. He replied, we shall. We might even make another movie together: he liked my new short novel I'd sent him in typescript, about Anna Freud and Hitler in Vienna 1912.

I was glad I wasn't in the movie world, where you could be intensely committed to an artistic project for a year, then told by a lawyer you were dismissed. It had happened to me when Geisler and Roberdeau sacked me as their screenwriter; but that had been for me a task, not a passion, as this project had become for Philippe.

In Flight Movie

I always become a child with learning difficulties on a plane. We were off to Toronto; I was flying in Business Class, Angela behind in Economy, since we could not expect Humber College, Toronto, to pay so much for my wife to come with me. She's not complaining – I, after all, am the old crock who needs to be able to stretch his legs out.

But it means she can't help me with the innumerable buttons on the sides of my seat. I've long since given up trying to watch a film. Even if I knew how the other passengers have miraculously sprouted their little TV monitors, I'd never cope with the earphones and finding the right button for sound. I'll just read. I'm deeply into another book about the Somme. I like reading about mammoth disasters on a flight – except airplane disasters. Needing to bring my quarter-inclined seat up straight, I fumble at the buttons and my seat hurls me violently back. At the same time, wishing to straighten my legs, I press a button which jerks my legs skywards. I look around me, hoping the others are ignoring my eccentric movements. They are.

My uncontrolled jerkings continue for about five minutes. At last I can read. Instantly the cabin lights are turned off for the movie.

I know there's a light high above me, but I have never succeeded in finding the right button to switch it on. Non-chalantly, as if I'm just idly drumming my fingers, I try various buttons, but none of them somehow works. Okay, I'll try to snooze: and repeat the process of mad seat-jerkings. I reflect that only a Cornish pisky would be able to read the seat-adjustment markings down by my thigh.

You might ask why I don't summon an attendant. Well, I don't know where the attendant-summoning button is. When the cabin crew are near me, they're too rushed giving out meal trays or drinks for me to be comfortable asking them; and once the lights are dimmed, they vanish. They're somewhere behind the screen, playing poker or having sex.

Besides, I don't like to confess that, having flown for the past forty years, I don't know where everything is.

Nearing the end of the long journey, the cabin falls completely silent as the plane starts to lose height. The sound of the engine diminishes, becomes almost silent itself, it's as if we were gliding. Through the window, away at the horizon, the flat, arid, brown-grey landscape of Ontario appears. Always at this stage I enter a mood of sadness, mirroring the dull-coloured flatness below us. I think how long I've been making this journey – almost every year since 1981. At first I came for the Harbourfront Literary Festival; later, for Humber. I feel sad, during the long, slow, silent descent because I see, like an internal landscape, all the changes and losses of my life since the first visit. In 1981 I was still living with Maureen in Hereford. I feel remorse for how I treated her, how little I appreciated her constant love and care, and how distant I was with Caitlin and Sean when they were children. Sean's first novel was not called *Absent Fathers* for no reason. Simultaneously and for years after, Denise and Ross the same. Later still, marriage to me made Victoria so unhappy she put on two stones, which she has now lost again. I feel the weight of remorse. *Agenbite of Inwit*, as Stephen Dedalus expressed it.

For a few years, following Denise's death, I was able to visit Ross and his wife Carrie, with her three children. Now he has moved out, moved away to Vancouver, where he's found a good job in computers and a much younger Russian-Jewish-Californian girlfriend. The relationship with an older, caring woman, which saved him during his mother's illness and after her death, became not what he needed a few years later.

I had seen he was stultifying, first in Shallow Lake, out in the wilderness of northern Ontario, and then in stolid Kitchener. He couldn't find a job, saw few people. He'd had a rotten adolescence, with Denise and me often rowing; the tragedy of the pool, when he had to dive into the murk and find Alex, my little grandson; Post-viral Fatigue Syndrome which kept him from school. Then his mother . . . Christ, I felt so sorry for him and so guilty. In Canada, becoming a house-husband, with no outlet for his wit, charm and intelligence, he felt, he said, as if he would go mad. He had never lived.

But there was Anna, the youngest of Carrie's three daughters. Aged seven now. Her own father had disowned her, wrongly believing she was Ross's offspring; she called Ross daddy and loved him as such. And he loved her intensely as a father. It broke his heart to leave her. But he had to leave, once the marriage had staled; he saved himself from despair, with great courage. But the price was Anna. Her mother wouldn't allow any contact, feeling it's better for Anna if she forgot him. I feel sad for Carrie too; she loved Ross deeply.

But as our plane seems to pick up speed, approaching the ground, my sadness becomes focused on that little girl. Her sudden loss, her unbearable pain. She's a sweet child. I imagine her drawing a picture, wanting to share it with her daddy, only she can't. I almost can't bear to think of her loneliness. And I know he almost can't bear it too.

We touch down, a feather-light landing. I wait for Angela in the landing-ramp. Half an hour later, in the open air, the hot, muggy air, I can smoke at last.

It was a good week. There are lovely people in the Humber Creative Writing program, who have become dear friends over the years. They feel the same way about me. With the visiting writers too there's a warm feeling of pleasant reunion. My workshop students are – as in most years – young, fresh and eager to learn. As usual the women greatly outnumber the men, and they're pretty. They warm to me, and I teach them well. Hey, I'm not such a bad guy! Just not much good at family life.

On the final evening, after we return to the plush hotel room from a meal out with fellow authors, Bruce J. Friedman and Alistair MacLeod, I engage in a lengthy phone conversation – interview, rather – with Susan Potter and her new director and co-scriptwriter Simon Monjack. Monjack has directed one film, *Two Days, Nine Lives* – not greeted enthusiastically by critics – with another about to be released, *Factory Girl.* He surprises me with his precise, rather academic Oxbridge voice. He tells me he loves my novel. He asks me probing questions about my vision of it. Susan intervenes occasionally with an off-the-wall comment and her hooting laugh. It's exactly two years since, in the same Park Hyatt hotel, she and I met Goldin.

Finance by September 3, straight into pre-production, and start shooting on October 23 . . . They've hired good casting people, who say they can find them the right actors ready to film in October, and also a whiz-bang PR company. They're no longer going to fly under the radar, but talk the project up.

> July 24 06
> *Susan Potter to Andrew Hewson*
> *Copy to Don Thomas . . .*

Dear Andrew: Thanks for the huge compliment, naming me a Giant Slayer. If I am, I feel it's because we are finally a team: Gabe and I with the unstoppable Simon . . . a genuine force of nature . . . who absolutely refuses to take NO for an answer. And his charming and beautiful fiancee, Danielle.

I attach a picture here of Simon and I signing his directing contract . . . about 10 days ago.

Never give up has always been my attitude, then my motto when my children teased me (years ago): 'Mom, you're like the little retarded girl in the movie of the week on tv: "Nevah give up . . . " ' – which one kid said in a retarded voice while hitting his chest with a limp fist.

Cheers, dear loyal and encouraging person!

Susan

Don Thomas to Andrew Hewson:

'I have been here before,
But how or when I cannot tell . . . '

– D. G .Rossetti

Andrew Hewson to Don Thomas:

Oh, absolutely.

Jesu, Maria

I relived your dying. No, that's not true; no one but yourself knows what your dying was like. I could not share it; I went along with you, but always guiltily and I suppose gratefully aware that it was you, not I, preparing to leave life.

But through a great work of art, I began to imagine I knew something of how you felt. It was *The Dream of Gerontius*, performed in Truro Cathedral as part of the St Endellion Summer Festival. Each summer, performers from all over the world come together to make music in the little village of St Endellion, with one major performance at Cornwall's cathedral. I've always loved *Gerontius* – truly, as Elgar said of it, 'This is the best of me' – but I hadn't listened to it for at least twenty years. This time, I knew I was ready to hear it again. We had unusually good seats, close to the performers, whom we could mostly see, but also with a TV monitor just above our heads.

From the unpredictable nature of the Festival, we didn't know what the quality of the performance would be. But from the first notes of the orchestra I knew they were excellent and that they were bringing an emotional commitment, beyond most professional orchestras playing the work as part of their routine repertoire. These musicians were breaking from their routine, enjoying beautiful Cornwall in sunny weather; and for pure pleasure making music. Already, from the first notes, I had a lump in my throat. Angela, who didn't know the work, whispered to me, 'This is magnificent'. Soon I could hardly hold the tears back.

When the tenor soloist began 'Jesu, Maria, I am near to death . . . And Thou art calling me . . . ' ' I was also with you in the hospice. So weak and helpless – you who had been so strong and forceful all your life – and paralysed below the waist. Saying goodbye to Ross with a brave smile; telling me your main grief was the thought of never seeing him, your mother or me again; I gently taking your very last cigarette from your fingers as the morphine took hold.

Now, listening to the intense music, I was afraid I would burst into tears; but managed just to hold them back. Then I felt an ache around my heart, Denise, and I wondered if I was about to have a heart attack. On a side-aisle, exposed to view, if I suddenly keeled over I would cause a sensation. The orchestra would see me; would they stop playing? 'I can no more; for now it comes again . . . That sense of ruin which is worse than pain . . . ' To die in the middle of a passionate account of *Gerontius* would be . . . wonderful? Altogether too theatrical?

The tension ache passed away, leaving me simply, and for the entire first part, close to tears.

I think the performance had so great an effect on me partly as an overspill from a barbecue three days earlier. An old friend had preached at length, with religious zeal, his anti-religious humanism, and his scorn for priests and ministers as hypocrites who could not possibly believe what they were proclaiming. Ever since, I'd been as it were rehearsing for *Gerontius* by singing, '*Proficiscere anima Christiana de hoc mundo . . .* ' Go

forth upon thy journey, Christian soul, from this world . . .
Hoping it's true, as you did, dying. Not believing but hoping.
And certainly convinced that this world, this universe, is
altogether more mysterious than humanism allows for. Life
may be, as Woody Allen said about casual sex, 'a shallow,
meaningless experience, but as shallow, meaningless
experiences go, it's one of the best.'   But I don't believe it's
meaningless; I believe uncertainly in God; and I believe the
words that Yeats put into the mouth of his character Crazy
Jane, 'All things remain in God'. In a year when atheism has
become chic, I believe more determinedly: *quia impossibile est.*

I suppose *Gerontius* contains the ultimate imaginary picture:
when the dead man is offered a glimpse of God in all His
awesome glory and cries 'Take me away, and in the lowest
deep there let me be . . . ' But I would rather believe in its
possibility than in my friend's bleak vision.

August 13

Susan: Are you still on course for getting the finance by
Sept 3, ready for a start on Oct 23?
    Don

Hi Don: So far, so good! Stay tuned.
    Susan

Our old dog knows nothing of this trivial matter. She
goes on with her special task of guarding the house against
marauders. When I was watching, mesmerized, the collapsing
Towers, the defining moment of our time, Tamsin plodded
into the living room, jumped up on the sofa (an athletic action
she can no longer perform), curled up and went to sleep.

After Christopher Smart . . .

For I will consider my dog Tamsin,
For she appeareth round the corner of the house
When we are drinking wine outside, then stops,
Forgetting why she appeareth there;
For she is 108 years old in human terms,
For she is almost blind and almost deaf,
Yet suddenly she trotteth down the garden,
For then her tail wags upon prink, in joy of living,
So that I have started to call her Baron von Trott;
For then she will slow up and plod around the house
Four or five times, defending it from marauders,
For she is small in size but mighty in spirit,
For when she stumbleth over a root, or her back legs
Won't work, she still goeth bravely forward;
For when we put some tasty fish in her dish,
She will slowly stir from her basket
And plod to her dish; but then she pauseth
For a long time, saying her prayers to the Lord,
Calling down blessing on the food,
Before suddenly stooping her head and
Snatching the fish hungrily.
For she kicketh out her legs in her dreams,
For she loveth to run on a beach,
And dreams of it later, many times,
Though she feareth the water.
For she is a happy little dog,
And teacheth how to grow old gracefully;
For she is the handmaid of the Lord,
And hath been loved by a Master and three Mistresses.
For she knoweth no other life but with us.

We Rock, We Roll

Would love another brief update, chere Susan.

Don

Hi Don: No problem, chere Don. We were on the front page of Variety on Friday!!! 8 paragraphs . . . unheard of for an independent picture. Alas, they did not credit me as the writer . . . just Simon.

We got constant calls all day . . . many from the major agents congratulating us on the big story . . . and making the grade . . . i.e., making it easier for them, which it does.

I found the story kind of churlish and negative: white noise, white elephant. It is press, and they did spell most of our names right . . . is what I'm being told.

So, dahlink . . . we're in the groove and seriously considering a couple of actresses – hoping for a big one, actually . . . but don't know if she can fit us in.

Anyway . . . we rock. We roll. We shall be victorious. We are not taking sloppy seconds on anything, nor no for an answer.

I'm sure there's more. Simon and I will go to Prague in a week or so. We are in constant conversation with Kevan Van Thompson, the line producer. The Chateau Ploskovice is quite wonderful, but lacks a ball room and a lake. We need another location to either take over, or fill in the blanks. Plus we need Odessa . . . which is why Latvia is mentioned.

Love on a Saturday night from me and Gabe,

Susan

Gradually Angela and I found, rather unexpectedly, that we are happily married. She is used to solitude, living alone, and never wanted to get married; I've always feared the claustrophobia of marriage. Yet we are happy.

I have been surprised by how kind and caring she is. She

gives off an air of being harder, and firmly does not wish to have children. But her nurturing instinct is strong. Not just to me – to Lucy, my new granddaughter, and Doris, Denise's lonely housebound mother. To Tamsin and Daisy, our elegant and coquettish black and white cat.

She is very tolerant of my gross manners. When I pick my nose and wipe away the snot secretly, hoping she hasn't noticed, she chuckles and says I am cute. When my lips grow reddled with wine, she chuckles and says I am cute. When I fart like a trumpet she chuckles and says I am cute. When my face grows covered with ice cream after the first lick of the cone, she chuckles and says I am cute. Nothing fazes her. Including my age.

I find calm with her – that calm which Pushkin said was essential to creation – but also excitement; and she with me. I worried at first about possible heart problems arising from over-strenuous sex; but so far her body has stood up to it. She chuckles when I quote this corny old joke to her. We enjoy laughter. As this evening . . . We're sitting out drinking wine, facing each other across the rustic picnic table; the sun sinking, the air warm but with a hint of autumn. 'I want to finish this book,' I say. She knows I've been waiting for the movie project to come to a head, one way or another. 'I wanted it to end with something decisive. But it's not going to happen.'

'You could send Susan some anthrax,' she suggests.

'Well, yes, I could do that!'

'Pretend it's from Geisler.'

'I'd have to send it from the States. From Texas; that's where his home is. "From Bobby with love".' We both laugh. 'No one would suspect me. I want her to make the film, everybody knows that. But Geisler . . . '

'He'd be in the slammer.'

I chuckle again, at the North Americanism. 'The slammer!'

'At least he'd have a home.'

'Well, that's true.'

'You could send her just enough to make her ill, then – '

'No, no, no! She'd have to die!'

'She'd have to die? Bobby would be on death row. He could get the electric chair.'

I almost choke on my gulp of wine. 'It would be a *cause célebre*. Imagine how many copies of my novel I'd sell!'

Susan relied on 'Jesus and wine'. For us, the best way of dealing with what seemed a huge gap between her (and presumably Simon's) optimism and their lack of progress was wine and black humour. Looking back, this exchange seems atrociously unfeeling; we bore no ill will to either Potter or Geisler; we both liked Susan, and for Bobby my affection remained constant.

The Little Matchstick Seller

'Hi Susan, I'm aware that the option agreement expires in ten days. And I wondered what your plans are.'

Hey Don! We have succeeded in extending the option with Goldin and Rubin. It took some doing, but he's good until October 25th. (Quoting Goldin: 'I'm making it longer than you asked for, because I'm a sweetie, but don't tell anyone.') I'll be receiving the extension docs from him tomorrow. We are able to pay on the option a smallish amount by September 12th, and that has definitely turned the tide . . . made it easier for Rubin to see that we are really real. We're working very diligently to have enough to make a payment to you, too, Don. So pray for cast . . . We have several large entities who have pledged their millions . . . the minute we get one or two names.

We are waiting to hear about Kirsten Dunst. (She's doing publicity for Marie Antoinette, and she may be tied up reshooting scenes or extra action stuff for Spiderman, so might not be available. Also, there may be a problem with her re: nudity . . . we hear. But you never know.)

So far we've generated over 200 articles on the Internet. Buzz, buzz, buzz. The MINUTE we get any negotiations going re: cast, our PR firm will put that out in the press, as well.

Just so you know, all of us – Gabe, me, Simon, Danielle (Simon's fiancee), Paul Campbell – our money finder and his wife – are ALL on this 200% 24/7 and counting!!!!!!!

Have heard nothing from Geisler. Thought we might, but with the last judgment against him on June 6, now registered with the copyright office (rec'd docs today!), wherein Goldin/ Rubin were awarded $6 mil in damages against Geisler . . . Barry thinks we will not be bothered by this person.

Anyway . . . this should cheer you up. I've taken my moniker (from Andrew) as Giant Slayer VERY SERIOUSLY. I love the role. Plus my old stand-bys: Jesus and wine. We shall overcome. We shall do this in plenty of time with plenty of money. Say Amen.

Much love,

Susan

Dear Susan: thanks for the update. Goldin is proving very amenable; you must have really charmed him.

'We're working very diligently to have enough to make a payment to you, too, Don.'

I feel it should be a priority. 'It's time!' as Pushkin says often in his poetry. *Porá!*

yours,

The little match-seller

Cut!

'I'm going to end it now,' I said to Angela, at the picnic table, on a fine late summer evening. 'My book is about *imaginary* pictures after all. It will always be an imaginary picture, even if, by a miracle of wine and Jesus, they make some low-budget movie. With actors the major studios don't want, picked up at the Hollywood Jobcentre. I'll finish it tonight. A lyrical ending, in our garden.' Tamsin is coming round the corner, then pauses, puzzled why she is there. Daisy is curled up near us, facing away, pretending she doesn't need us. 'Yes, I'll end it now. Tamsin and Daisy enjoying the evening. You and I face to face.'

'Denise's spirit in the flowers.'

'Many spirits.' I raised my glass. I seemed to see people who were never here in this garden: Margaret Hewson, John Roberdeau; and one who was here just once, the man of sorrows Bobby Geisler. I can't condemn him in any 'last judgement' (Susan's words in a different context.) 'Judge not that ye be not judged', and all that.

'Of course.'

I refilled Angela's glass. Smiling, she placed two fingers on her left shoulder, our private signal in company that I have wine smeared round my mouth. I wiped my mouth with a tissue. Just as the sun breaks through some low cloud, and late summer and late day warmth floods through, I lift my face, close my eyes and exclaim, 'The sun! The sun!'

'It's a beautiful evening.'

'A good place to end *Bleak Hotel*.'

'The sun just going behind the trees . . . '

'The bread, the pâté.'

'The Tesco wine.'

'The book of verse.'

She nods towards the open window. 'Bryn Terfel singing.'

'It's not paradise but good enough! *Cut!*'

We have a Movie Now!

I changed my mind on looking at my computer screen at the end of the evening, because – well, because Potter was obviously *convinced* there would soon be a film. She had e-mailed to say she was in Chicago, having risen at 1.30 a.m. to get to the airport; and later would be flying back to LA. She'd gone to Chicago to 'talk to money'.

What energy, in a woman of sixty! One couldn't deny her passion and commitment.

She and Simon, she went on, would be flying to Prague on September 11 (an ominous date to be flying) to join the pre-production team there *who had already started*. She still believed the cameras could roll within eight weeks. Possibly a movie without actors. They'd just sent out offers to Anne Hathaway, Robert Downey Jr., Colin Firth and Rupert Friend. There were surely more stars and starlets in this non-movie than any other non-movie in history.

It had to be madness. *Folie de l'Hotel Blanc.* But I would hold on to see what happened. A little longer.

Sept 3 06
Another long e-mail in which she said the Czech people would soon have a site location schedule drawn up, which would allow us – Angela and I and my daughter Caitlin – to plan our visit according to what we'd like to see. Exteriors first, then interiors. She was praying for unseasonably good weather. Babi Yar to be shot after Christmas, she thought.

I'd told her once, only half-jokingly, that I'd like a walk-on role, *à la* Hitchcock. She asked me now to think about it, because they'd have to plan costume and make-up for me.

God, they had to be really confident! They wanted to plan *my* little appearance! Without finance, without money, with the million and one things she had to do to get this movie up and running, she was going to talk to a dressmaker to make me up a costume . . . I responded that I had always dreamed of being a lecherous hotel guest, climbing stairs, and goosing a chambermaid coming down. But that I was flexible.

Simon, she repeated, was the great new source of energy. He was helping her to revise the screenplay, and keeping them to a firm timetable.

September 19

Hi Don: Simon has wooed a wonderful actress, Vera Farmiga, who really really wants to play the lead in our film. Her agent and manager are thrilled for her. She usually loses parts to Rachel Weisz . . . and as the *NY Times Sunday Magazine* cover story says, She deserves great roles, because she's such a great actress . . . but there are so few lead roles for women. Unlike Meryl Streep's time when she was actually able to build a career.

I'm attaching a picture of Vera and the NY Times article. Vera is an actors' actor and everyone at the agencies is excited . . . meaning it's easier to attach the men now that we have this lovely woman for our lead.

Also, attached, see the picture of Rupert Friend.

WE HAVE A MOVIE NOW!

Geoffrey Rush may do Freud. And we're going out to Javier Bardem to play Victor.

All good news. Leaving for Prague on Saturday. Simon to follow on Monday, as the boots are on the ground there working away. Our first week schedule includes going off with the Location Manager and the Production Designer to finalize locations.

Best, Susan

Allowing myself just a little excitement, I googled Vera Farmiga and was struck by how perfect her face was for Lisa. Moreover, I learned that she had Ukrainian parents and could not speak English till she was six. Perfect! Lisa was Ukrainian. I e-mailed Potter enthusiastically.

Sept. 27

Geisler emerged, a leviathan from the deeps, copying me a long, often repeated e-mail proclaiming his rights, this time sent to the journalist who wrote the article 'White Noise'. There was one addition – Geisler said he'd heard Potter and Monjack had abandoned their project. Slightly alarmed, I e-mailed Susan. Within a few hours her response came . . .

> All good. Geisler lies.
> Leaving for Prague this weekend.
> Casting news is that Anne Hathaway needs another day or so to think. Emmy Rossum is a FOR SURE should Anne pass.
> CAA loves us.
> We shall have more to tell you soon.
> Xxx Susan

Disturbed by the sudden disappearance of Vera Farmiga, and sure Susan was not yet in Prague, I rang her on her cellphone. She sounded a bit shaky, unsure at first who I was. Yes, she was still in California, 'flying to Prague at the weekend'. Starting date had been put back to November 14. All was well, except she was uncertain whether the world is good or evil. Then came her Ethel Merman laugh: 'Of course it's both!' I said, 'You sound a bit shaky.' 'No, I've just come in from walking the dog with Gabe. I'll keep you informed.'

> Dear Susan: I'm confused . . . This is what you wrote a week ago . . .
> 'Simon has wooed a wonderful actress, Vera Farmiga, who really really wants to play the lead in our film. Her agent and manager are thrilled for her.'

And she did really look the part, even to the Ukrainian connection. Yet today it's Anne H. again, with Emmy Rossum in reserve. So Vera is not even the reserve any more? Did she back out? Did she tear away from Simon's (metaphorical) kisses crying 'No! No! I can't!'?

You did sound rather troubled on the phone, as if you're having a hard time. Hope all turns out well.

love,

Don

Sept 28

I am working 18–20 hour days to make this happen. I'm scared stiff most of the time . . . but then someone makes me laugh.

We are now out to find bridge financing until the big draw down. All financing for making the movie comes from people investing when you have stars. We never had stars. Now we have lesser stars, and maybe some bigger name men.

It is cut and paste every day. Both with money and with talent. My jaw will not unclench. I hate my bras. I can't sleep. I feel like throwing up in the morning. And fuck all: it's only a goddamn movie . . . right?

Our casting directors and Simon/me had a contretemps. They pushed Vera, told her she had the job, when we were still waiting for a meeting with Anne Hathaway . . . which had been set up. They told the agents of Anne that Simon was not avail. on Friday. He was. I called back and got him his meeting. He loved Anne . . . she him. We thought, great . . . a choice. We had to run it out. Then Emmy Rossum entered the picture. Then Vera's people and Vera got angry. WE apologized all over the place. The casting directors quit. So, yesterday I'm in LA half the day meeting with another casting director. This morning I have to get her ALL the files. We carry on.

I don't know how this helps you, but you wanted to know.

'What gave Geisler the idea you'd closed down the project?'

I am not privy to the workings of the brain of such a person.

'What's happened to the payment to me that you firmly hoped would come in September?'

No one has been paid. It's ugly. I apologize. I'm doing EVERYTHING I can to make this happen. We were supposed to have a war chest of half a million. We had a finder for this. He fell short by 1/2 a mil. Ergo, I didn't get paid and neither did many others.

With cast we can move forward more rapidly. I finally have someone swinging the big deals – The Collective's Shaun Redick. Great guy. He found me a new Casting Director yesterday. We carry on.

Emmy Rossum will do the picture. We're running the foreign sales numbers today . . . seeing which is better Vera or Emmy. We think we might have a shot with Vera. Her agent called and I apologized. Look for me, I'll be the one in the little black pyjamas cow towing.

my best,

Susan

Principal Photography

It's an emotional reunion with Denise . . .

She is very upset, crying. Can't go on like this any more. I do my best to calm her. Is it because of Christmas coming? It was always stressful on Christmas Day in Hereford; I needed to be in two houses. I'd compromise by having dinner at home with Maureen and our kids, then have supper with Denise and Ross. Now I tell her we could spend the whole of Christmas together, in Carnkie, with my aunts Nellie and Cecie and

Uncle Eddie. But I warn her Cecie's roasts are not great. Or we could go and stay at a hotel, in Falmouth, say, or on the Scillies. Could even go abroad, but I'm not sure we can afford it.

We go upstairs at the Coach House, and along to my study. The Coach House is like a stone ship, long and slender; my study is at the prow. There's a mattress on the floor and we're going to make love. But my wife (I'm not sure which one) follows us, and engages me in an awkward conversation about domestic trivia. She eventually leaves, but the mood is spoiled, as she'd wanted. We don't make love. Denise is leaving me, this is insupportable.

Downstairs again, a youngish man called Marcus has called to see her; or perhaps to take her away. I conceive a desperate plan for the three of us to live together, here in the Coach House. It's quite big enough. But even as the idea comes to me it goes. A phone rings; she moves quickly to answer it, as if she knows it's a new lover. My heart sinks. Roger, our Hereford friend, gets there first and picks up the phone. Denise hovers, expectant, as does Ross. I feel sick with fear. She 's going to leave any moment, and I'll never see her again. I don't know where she's living, don't have her phone number.

At the last moment, left alone with her, I ask her where she's teaching. She's not teaching, she says, she's taking some special course. With many attractive, lecherous male tutors, I tell myself. Other people move into the room – Marcus, Roger, his wife Cath . . . Desperate for some space, I push Denise down the corridor of my Hereford house, towards the study Maureen and I had built on at the back of our little semi. I push her up against a wall, and at last smell her scent and feel her warmth, her breath. She puts her arms around me. I sob with relief, telling her how much I love her. She softens, murmuring, 'I'll phone you tomorrow'. So we're still together! It's not 'I'll give you a call sometime', it's 'I'll phone you tomorrow': it's not over, thank God! She still anticipates we'll be in touch every day. 'You wouldn't rather I phoned you?' 'No,' she replies, decisively but almost tenderly, 'I'll call you.'

Our movie goes on! It doesn't require finance, or actors. Only ourselves. The budget is limitless and nothing. It's a major movie. And a fantastic one. With many atmospheric scenes, such as that opening in the murky restaurant; the sudden dramatic terror of her pursuit of me through a hospital; the opening out to Latvia, with the close escape from death thanks to her shock exposure of her cunt; the equally shocking appearance of an old crone, as I open my eyes in our cabin, expecting Denise and tender lovemaking; walking hand in hand through Red Square, the domes sparkling; the recurrent fear of losing her, not knowing where she is, who she's with; the moments of sudden joy, in a passionate kiss, the scent of her hair and skin close to mine . . . It's confused and wild and surreal, as our life together was.

The latest from Hollywood was that Geoffrey Rush had agreed to play Freud. They were pursuing Penelope Cruz as Lisa. They were now going for up and coming actors, who wouldn't screw them around. Start date was pushed back to January 10 2007, on a reduced budget. It would be an art movie; all of us would have to take less money, Susan warned.

Apparently the problem with actresses is they don't want to take their clothes off. Or their agents don't want them to. I responded that they don't need to take their clothes off, there can be erotic play with half-undress. Susan countered that they don't even want to show a gleam of breast. It's all a surprise to me. I hadn't realised all the Hollywood actresses had turned Islamic.

I asked her why didn't they approach Tilda Swinton again. She'd had a problem, according to Potter, with Philippe as director; but now he was gone. She replied that Tilda was far too old – forty-eight. She and Simon had changed the script to make Lisa, at first, young and glamorous.

Angela and I flew to Vienna for the start of a week's cruise on the Danube. Just a couple of months ago we had thought we might prolong our trip to watch the first day of principal photography – fixed for a while at November 1. Now I simply 'forget it all a while / Upon a woman's breast', and upon an incredibly unblue (even in unseasonable sunshine) Danube. Often on foreign holidays I don't feel much sexual energy; it's too hot, or the beds too narrow, or the atmosphere too claustrophobic; but this time I do. There's a potent aphrodisiac – the fact that Angela is the only youthful passenger among 180 of us old gaffers. She is unique too in dressing with chic, stockinged, high-heeled elegance. A girly womanly female feminine dame, as the grossly sexist song from *South Pacific* put it. I see all the doddery old men with doddery old wives trying to hide their wistful desire for her and their insane hatred of me – and that feels great.

I imagine, on the MS Johann Strauss, while Angela lounges across from me in a jacuzzi, that I really am watching a scene from *The White Hotel* being filmed. The set, a hotel terrace, is high up on a snowy mountain, and the terrace tables bear crockery and thermos flasks. The people sitting there, drinking cups of tea, are the merry folk of my youth, the 'aunts' and 'uncles' of Carnkie.

'Donald!' I hear a woman's voice exclaim. I turn and recognise Iris Prisk, the much older sister of my first wife Maureen. Silver-haired and buxom.

'Iris!'

She rises and offers me her cheek to kiss. 'How *are* you, my handsome!'

'Fine. I didn't expect *you* here!'

I can see others I recognise, who smile at me and nod greetings. All those lovely working people from the scarred mining landscape: stout Mrs Waters, with her pretty daughter Rosemary; Percy Kemp, the chapel organist, Mrs Adams, Audrey Oates, Mrs Webb . . . their singsong voices chirp like a cloud of insects, never stopping.

'Well, we didn't expect to *be* here,' Iris says; 'but when this nice American lady wrote to us, we were some proud of 'ee! And your Mum and Dad would be some proud of 'ee. What could we do? We hired a Marigold coach from Lanner and here we are, goin' to be in a film!'

Audrey Oates, attractive, cherry-lipsticked, rose and kissed me on the cheek. 'Some lovely hotel, i'n it, Donald?'

'It's not real.'

'Well, that don't matter.'

All around us, I can see that people – familiar people – have produced packs of cards; they are busy trumping each other. Probably Susan has warned them there could be a lot of waiting around. Percy says, 'Why's that l'il maid over there exposing her chest like that?'

I look around to where, in a corner of the terrace, with a jagged white peak in the background, cameras are clustered round the main actors. And the star actress is hardly a *little* maid. Ah, so she changed her mind!

'It's in my book.'

He winces, and goes on gazing. 'I suppose we have to move with the times.'

'Are mum and dad here?'

'Of course! Somewhere!' Audrey says. But I can't see them. Nor auntie Cecie, Uncle Eddie . . . Yet they have to be here. Everyone is at the white hotel.

A rumour, a murmur, runs excitedly around the tables that they must queue up to suck at Kate Winslet's nipples.

'My gar!' Iris exclaims. 'Why should we do *that*, Donald?'

'Well, that's in my book too.'

Soon a long queue of those good Methodists is snaking

around the tables. Others are in no hurry; some start to play 'Shake-a-leg', as in the old Sunday School socials. Three of the women sit in a line, a blanket over their laps. The 'victim' – I recognise the piggy face of Mrs Waters – goes along the line of six legs, saying to each one in turn, 'Shake a leg!' and taking hold of it. The fifth leg – it could be any – a pillow encased in a stocking – comes away in her hands, to shrieks of laughter. Then Mrs Waters has to go and suck at Kate's ample breast.

I see old Evie Tresidder, black-frocked and sun-wizened, rocking on her seat. She says, 'Donald, how are you, my lover?'

'I'm fine, Auntie Evie.'

'I remember the day you was born! May Kemp came up the road and told us your mum had a baby, and I said to her, "Does the cheel have a spout, or no?" And May said, "Ess, 'ee do 'ave a spout right enough!" '

My gaze keeps returning to the milky scene. A man, whose name I can't recall, calls out to another, as he stoops to a nipple: 'I 'ope 'tis better milk than yours, Everson!' to general laughter.

Bald, hawk-nosed Everson Wills shouts, 'But it isn't pasteurized, that's for sure!' and his right eyelid twitches.

'Bet you won't be milkin' this udder by machine, Everson!' calls Cuthbert Johns, from the wheelchair that had prevented him serving in the war, before a sudden miracle on VJ Day restored full vigour to his legs.

Again the twitch from Everson's eye. 'You're bleddy right, Cuthbert! It's a mouth-job, this one!' to another universal shriek of merriment.

Just then the chatter is stilled; eyes are looking towards the sky; even Percy Kemp, the organist, takes his mouth from Winslet's breast to stare up: something that is like, but not quite like, a bat is darting and weaving around, high up. 'By Christ!' says Willie Harris, removing his Players Weight from his lips. 'It's a bleddy womb! Is it yours, Edna?'

'No, it's not mine!' Edna calls. 'I still got mine! Not much good to me, but I still got'n.'

We may have to Move On

Arriving home, I found a recorded message from Andrew Hewson, saying a Hollywood producer had called him, asking for confirmation that the film rights to *The White Hotel* had reverted to Barry Goldin on October 29. Andrew had declined to confirm or deny. 'We may find we have to move on', he concludes his message.

Nov 1

Dear Susan: I hear rumours that the rights reverted to Goldin on Oct 29. Is this so? If it is, it's a crying shame, and a terrible blow to us all.

Love,

Don

Susan to Don
Copy to Barry Goldin

Hi Don: Legally speaking, that's true . . . but I did pay him $65,000 and there's $35k owing, which I'm working on getting together

There was some fallout due to a person trying to work around me. This person said they'd paid Goldin . . . and then didn't . . . waited to the last minute to offer to buy me out. If this person could have gotten the movie made, I would have acquiesced. They cannot.

I have Goldin's understanding that this is what went down, and he knows I'm working on it. He's a good guy and able to work with me, give me some flexibility.

All very scary, to be sure. But I'm very close to having a better deal than I've ever had.

xx Susan

We Rock, We Roll

Nov 2

Hi Don: The rumours turned out to be correct. Simon Monjack swept in and gave Goldin '6 figures', which I'm guessing is $100k. Then he's planning on rewriting the script so nothing remains of my contribution, he says. Impossible, since he'd have to leave out everything from the novel that I used in my original adaptation . . . and leave out whatever Simon and I wrote together: together means the script with both our names on it, whether he wrote it by himself or not . . .

Now he owns it. He can make it all by himself. It's only a matter of his finding the money. That's where I come in . . . This has been my whole life for over two years. So I soldier on . . . can't eat, drink myself to sleep. Now to keep from starving (good thing I can't eat) and keep a roof over my head (I have NO money and am behind in rent and utilities) – I will grovel and bring as much to the table as I possibly can this week! We have no one left to borrow from. I've been played like a fiddle. Fucked like a jail house bitch.

Pray for miracles! Pray they abound! Call down all the forces in heaven and on earth!!

Love,

Susan

I read this, and saw its black humour – even though it spelt the end of my contract with JOA Productions and therefore of all hope of some money eventually. Monjack, her saviour for whom she'd dropped Mora, 'the unstoppable' Simon, the 'force of nature', who 'wouldn't take no for an answer', had taken over!

For Susan, it was a huge dream smashed to pieces. I felt very sorry for her, as I had done for Philippe. Her presence had always warmed me, because of her zany vitality and generosity of spirit. I felt sorry too for investors who had bought into her dream, including an old lady from her church who, according to Susan, had invested her life savings.

Goldin told Bernie Nyman that Potter had alienated every-one, and they'd been urging him to get rid of her. Certainly she was an unorthodox operator, but there should surely be room for a woman of passion and idealism in the movie business. He refused to tell Bernie who now held the option – even though he must have known Potter had told me – nor for how long. He 'advised' me not to have any more contact with Potter.

I heard a whisper that Goldin had ordered Monjack to send to him any e-mails or correspondence from me.

It's wonderful to be trusted.

I received friendly greetings from Monjack through his assistant, but my repeated requests for a short e-mail from him, or a five-minute phone call, to tell me about his plans, went unanswered. I guessed he was under orders not to tell me anything. If he actually, by miracle, made the film, I wondered if it would be at a secret location.

Strenue ac fideliter.

Dec 19 2006

Geisler emerged, in the form of a copied e-mail to an agent, asking if he still represented Brittany Murphy, and was she still negotiating to star in *the White Hotel*. If so, Geisler thought he should read his letter to 'Variety' of September 27, which he attached. He ended the short e-mail by saying he was feeling stronger, walking again if only hesitantly, and with a cane.

Brittany Murphy, h'mm? Another amazing Lisa.

Apparently – I was left picking up rumours – Goldin was suing Susan Potter in a New York court, perhaps seeking to forestall any attempt by her to freeze potential film production by litigation against him or Monjack. Goldin, contacting Nyman, wanted me to hand over to him any e-mails I'd received from Potter since the beginning of September, He also attached a letter to Rick Knight, 'the very parfit gentle knight', asking him to appear in a Memphis court to assist him in the suit against Paul Verner, Geisler's former attorney.

Nyman advised that I should hand over the Potter e-mails. I asked him to tell Goldin I was overwhelmed by deadlines and the demands of family and Christmas, but would attend to his request as soon as possible. Goldin had informed Knight that he would be unable to travel in the next month as his thirteen year old daughter was awaiting a major operation. I offered my sympathy, and the hope that all would be well. I thought sadly of that unknown teenager, in her pain and fear; and how far from her small and precious world was the vast legal web that her father had partly spun, in the service of his client, partly been caught up in. She and the *White Hotel* movie war were about the same age.

Another Pushkin quotation: 'There is no happiness outside of the ordinary.' It seemed, somehow, even more absurd and irrelevant that the legal *tsunami* continued to roll on, from shore to shining shore.

A Surprise Ending

We are out sailing on a lake that nestles between the mountains. It's a beautiful day. A bright blue sky and the white hotel gleaming, half way up the snow-covered mountain. The old villagers are having a great time, snapping with their box cameras, taking part in impromptu bingo, drinking lemonade, chatting merrily, or just stretched out in deck-chairs, drawing in the sun.

All of them scrupulously avoid staring at Kate Winslet and Dustin Hoffman, who are being filmed in furtive coupling. Winslet sits astride Dustin, her long dress spread over them.

Suddenly Willie Harris takes yet another Players Weights from his lips to exclaim, 'By Christ! the hotel's on fire!'

Everyone becomes silent and motionless, gazing at the shore.
'you're bleddy right!' Everson says.

'Oo, *'ell!'* mutters Ken Penhaligon.

'Donald, isn't that awful!' Audrey says.

Percy Kemp: 'It's a gonner.'

Everson: 'That was your cigarette butt, Willie; I see'd 'n
smokin' away. I 'ope you're not goin' to get sued for that.'

'It's alright,' I say; 'it's made of cardboard. There's no one
there.'

'*And the winner of the special award for the best imaginary picture
of the last twenty five years is . . . THE WHITE HOTEL!'*
(Tumultuous applause. Author makes his way up, to the
tune of 'Clap Hands Here Comes Charlie')

THOMAS: 'I'm lost for words. This is a great honour. More
than eighty years ago, Hollywood took my parents to its
heart, and now it's taken me. There are many people I
would like to share this award with . . . Terry Malick, for his
interest in Mizoguchi, which prompted Geisler and Roberdeau to workshop *Sancho the Bailiff*; Geisler and Roberdeau
themselves for their unorthodox financial management;
Isabella Rossellini, for ending her relationship with David
Lynch; Tony Blair and NATO for attacking Serbia; Horst
Danning, for his traumatic fall and coma – I'm so glad he's
recovered fully; and Barry Goldin and Gerry Rubin for
tying the project up in litigation for several years . . .
(*Applause.*) . . . Without their contribution, this would not
have been the fine imaginary picture it is . . . I mustn't forget
the amazing actors who have taken part in it . . . I see many
of you here tonight . . . Meryl, Barbra, Nicole, Tony,
Dustin, Juliette, Tilda, Kate, Javier, Vera, Monica, Jeremy,
Emmy, Hilary, Milla, Colin, Penelope, Rupert, Robert,
Bruno, Anne, Brittany, Geoffrey . . . So many more. Has
there ever been such a glittering cast? And the team of

directors – Bernardo, the two Davids, Pedro, Mark, Philippe, Hector, Emir . . . My God, how could we fail, with such a multitude of talents? (*Applause*.) . . . You know, forty years ago a clairvoyant told me I would one day die in California. I've consequently avoided it like the plague! (*Laughter*.) But your nomination tempted me here, and so far I'm still – '

I suddenly, unexpectedly, had a surprise ending for my book: that I really didn't care if the film got made or not.

Neither delight nor disappointment, but indifference. It had engendered too much hatred, vengefulness, duplicity, greed, hysteria. '*Frankly, my dear, I don't give a damn.* ' Or rather, there was positive pleasure in the thought of Goldin and Rubin being unable to find anyone to make the film, and therefore, eventually, having to see the rights revert to me, or to my heirs.

Then, if I was still on this earth, I would offer the rights, for five hundred dollars, to a young, photogenic Serbian actress who, for the last couple of years, had been intermittently pouring out to me in e-mails her longing to play Lisa, or even to direct the movie. She would make it on a pathetic budget, and it would probably be not very good, but she would make it with passion. And no one would sue her, or me. We would watch its first showing in a small, dingy cinema in Belgrade, and afterwards our party would drink and smoke in a bar till the early hours.

From the Sidelines

I have watched, amused, from the sidelines as the black farce has continued. Legally there appeared to be deadlock; with everyone suing everyone – possibly even themselves. Geisler too was wandering mysteriously from place to place, still from time to time assuring the world that he alone had the right to produce the movie.

I heard rumours that Monjack was living with his proposed 'star', Brittany Murphy.

Next, in an issue dated June 4, 2007, though coming out in late May, the *National Enquirer* published a piece by John South headlined '**Brittany Murphy's Hubby Faces 3 Arrest Warrents**', sub-headed 'Alleged con man could be deported'. None of South's allegations, concerning 'green card' immigration rights and financial matters, has to my knowledge been substantiated; but certainly Monjack and Murphy had got married. According to the *N.E.* reporter, Murphy's publicist had told him it took place 'in a Jewish ceremony at her home'.

In August 2007 Potter and Monjack issued a short statement saying that the latter had withdrawn from the project; Potter would continue to pursue it. They wished each other well. Murphy had also withdrawn. I don't know what legal negotiations might or might not lie behind the brief statement. But Potter was left without an option, and it seemed to me even more absurdly unlikely that Rubin/Goldin would find a production team willing, with pure generosity, to hand over three million dollars to them before they could even start on the tainted project.

A year later, so far as I am aware, still no director had been appointed. But somewhere in the Alps there is a rather splendid hotel where . . .